D0048738

TIME TO WEEP

by

STEPHEN HILL

CREATION
HOUSE
Orlando   FL

TIME TO WEEP by Stephen Hill
Published by Creation House
Strang Communications Company
600 Rinehart Road
Lake Mary, FL 32746
Web site: http://www.creationhouse.com

This book or parts thereof may not be reproduced in any form, stored
in a retrieval system, or transmitted in any form by any means—
electronic, mechanical, photocopy, recording, or otherwise—without
prior written permission of the publisher, except as provided by
United States of America copyright law.

Unless otherwise noted, all Scripture quotations are from the New
American Standard Bible. Copyright © 1960, 1962, 1963, 1968, 1971, 1972,
1973, 1975, 1977 by the Lockman Foundation. Used by permission.

Scripture quotations marked KJV are from
the King James Version of the Bible.

Scripture quotations marked NIV are from the Holy Bible,
New International Version. Copyright © 1973, 1978, 1984, International
Bible Society. Used by permission.

Scripture quotations marked NKJV are from the New King James
Version of the Bible. Copyright © 1979, 1980, 1982 by Thomas
Nelson, Inc., publishers. Used by permission.

Background photo provided by Photo Disc., Inc., Copyright © 1997.
Photo of man weeping provided by Cathy Woods.

Copyright © 1996 by Stephen Hill
All rights reserved

Library of Congress Catalog Card Number: 97-65655
International Standard Book Number: 0-88419-459-0

89012345 BBG 987654
Printed in the United States of America

*To Jeri, my beloved wife,
loving mother of our children,
my constant companion
and co-laborer in the
harvest fields.*

ACKNOWLEDGMENTS

To my mother, Ann E. Hill, who fought the battle with travailing tears. Thanks for never giving up on your son

Special thanks to Larry Art, Veronica Rosas and Tomi Davidson for all your transcribing and valuable editorial assistance.

Grateful appreciation to Leonard and Martha Ravenhill, both weeping warriors, for your prayers and constant encouragement. Thank you for not just pointing the way, but leading the way. Reverend Ravenhill received his reward before the completion of this book. His epitaph summarizes the life of this dear servant of Christ: "Are the things you are living for worth Christ dying for?"

Thank you, Winkie Pratney, for your simple rules on writing and for taking the time to help a fellow soldier.

Special thanks to Scott Sawyer, for your hours of editorial labor and for always having a kind, uplifting word.

To Reverend John Kilpatrick and the congregation of Brownsville Assembly of God, Pensacola, Florida, for your continued intercessory prayer with travailing tears. You have touched the heart of God.

To everyone who supports us in our missions work around the world, we send a hearty "God bless you!"

CONTENTS

FOREWORD

I first visited Brownsville Assembly of God in March 1996, nine months after revival erupted there. I had heard the exciting reports about how the church — a typical Pentecostal congregation in Pensacola, Florida — had experienced a visitation of the Holy Spirit in June 1995.

Charisma magazine had already published one report explaining that the unusual movement began during a Father's Day service when a young evangelist named Steve Hill preached. Services were scheduled four nights a week in the church's twenty-three hundred-seat sanctuary, and within weeks overflow rooms with video monitors had to be provided for the huge crowds. Thousands of people — including scores of teenagers who had been involved in drugs, street gangs and witchcraft — had made decisions for Christ at Brownsville Assembly's altar.

As I flew to Pensacola from Orlando, prepared to write another report for the magazine, I recognized a deep longing in my heart to do more than just witness a revival or tell others about it. I wanted to experience it myself. So I broke one of the fundamental rules of journalism and decided that I would not just be an objective observer when I arrived at Brownsville Assembly. I wanted to be involved in the story.

Lord, I prayed under my breath on the airplane, *please touch me, too. I need revival myself.* I would soon learn how eager the Holy Spirit was to answer that prayer.

A tangible sense of the presence of God electrified the crowd inside the church that night. I learned that some of the visitors had arrived as early as two o'clock that afternoon to reserve a seat. They came hungry for a touch from God. Some of them had driven from Canada and Indiana to find spiritual renewal and refreshment. I would later learn that the seven long-haired teenagers seated on the front row were collectively called "the chain of grace" because they each found Christ during the course of about a month after a friend witnessed to them.

As I looked around the auditorium and observed thousands of hands raised in worship, I said to myself, *This must be what genuine revival looks like.* After I heard Steve Hill preach his soul-searing message about the urgency of the hour, and as I witnessed hundreds of people streaming to the altar — many of them in tears — I was sure that real revival had begun.

I knew this was genuine revival not just because I felt the holiness of God in the room, or because people were literally convulsing as they fell to their knees in front of the podium. I knew it because my own heart was laid bare by an invisible sword as Steve humbly shared from the Scriptures. His message was not hype; it wasn't some eloquent attempt to whip people into an emotional frenzy; he wasn't manipulating people with his delivery. His words were simply bathed in God's power, and it melted all human resistance. Including mine.

Later that evening, I fell on my knees in a back corner of the auditorium at Brownsville. Through uncontrollable sobs I asked the Lord to fill me with His Spirit in a fresh way. I turned over to him a heavy burden I was carrying about a broken relationship in my past. And with a fresh desire to yield every part of my being to Him, I told God He could do whatever He wanted with my career, my talents, my marriage, my income, my children and even my weaknesses.

That was the beginning of a new chapter in my walk with the Lord. After two more days in Pensacola, I went home convinced that something eternal had been sparked inside of me that was growing into a flame.

Not long after I returned home, I had an unusual experience in the middle of the night. I woke up with an uncanny awareness that I had been praying in my sleep for my pastor and his two teenage sons, yet I knew that these prayers did not originate in my mind or from any knowledge I had of my pastor's family. The prayers were coming from deep within me, from my spirit — as if they were the thoughts and deep concerns of the Holy Spirit Himself. As soon as I realized this, I remembered the words of the apostle Paul in Romans 8:26:

> In the same way, the Spirit helps us in our weakness. We do not know what we ought to pray for, but the Spirit himself intercedes for us with groans that words cannot express. And he who searches our hearts knows the mind of the Spirit, because the Spirit intercedes for the saints in accordance with God's will (NIV).

Over the next few weeks I realized that God was teaching me something fundamental about prayer as a result of my encounter with Him in Pensacola. For so many years of my Christian life I had approached prayer as a totally human activity. I had made my lists of wants and needs; I had asked God to do what I wanted Him to do; I had prayed my will and not His.

Suddenly I realized that a deeper level of prayer and communion with the Father exists — a realm He wants us all to experience. I began to understand that He wants to pray through me; He wants His own passions, burdens and holy desires to be expressed when I intercede. As this truth became a revelation to me, my prayer life began to involve more listening, less talking and a quest for true humility. I realized that when I come into God's presence, it is not to tell Him what to do; it is to agree with what He is already doing.

When I returned to Pensacola in July 1996 for a second visit, I sat near a group of intercessors who typically pray for the lost who come to the meetings each night. In the middle of the service, one woman was quietly bowed over with her head between her knees, and I could hear her as she groaned faintly. Another woman seated nearby was weeping as she rocked back and forth. A third woman eventually rolled out of her seat into the floor as she prayed intensely.

Had I not had my own experience with groaning in the Spirit, I might have thought these women were putting on a show of emotionalism. But I understood immediately what was happening. They had yielded themselves to the Holy Spirit, and He was praying through them. They felt His compassion for lost souls; His tears became theirs; they felt perhaps just a tiny percentage of the grief God feels when someone willingly turns away from Him and chooses to reject Jesus.

Like those women I watched that night at Brownsville, Steve Hill has asked God to weep through him. He has been gripped by a supernatural sense of God's love for the church and for unbelievers. And he wants all Christians to experience the Holy Spirit in the deepest way possible. In this crucial hour, I hope all of us will listen to the message God has placed in this man's heart. And I pray that all of us will allow the Spirit to weep through us.

J. Lee Grady, executive editor
Charisma magazine

INTRODUCTION

T his is a book about tears. In a cynical and calloused culture like ours, we have forgotten how to cry. Our high-tech society is sorely in need of a supernatural high-touch.

I was in Haight-Asbury the "day the music died" — when the hippies themselves took a big coffin down the streets and officially buried the hippie movement. The Age of Aquarius came, the "moon was in the seventh house, Jupiter aligned with Mars," and nothing happened! The dream fell apart at the seams. What went wrong? The young of the previous generation knew how to dance, they knew how to laugh and they knew how to sing. But they never learned how to cry.

Some of the authors of the old rock classics understood. Love can mean pain; love can mean separation; and love certainly can mean tears.

Yet, the central metaphor of Generation X is pain. Mourning black is the color of choice for the largest generation in America's history

— the thirteenth generation that has inherited a black hole of broken promises, broken hopes and broken dreams. If ever a world needed to know the redeeming power of tears, it is this one.

Stephen Hill is not a sad man. As one of the most passionate and dedicated missionary evangelists I know, he is one who burns with a love for Jesus and for people. That joyous intensity comes out of his very eyes when you talk to him about Christ and when Steve speaks of the Lord's awesome visitations in his life and ministry. But Steve has seen the other side of salvation. He, like his Master, knows of the price of joy set before him. Stephen Hill has gone out "weeping, bearing precious seed," and the astonishing harvests in his life are evidence of the strong and tender secret he shares with you in this book.

To the prophet Ezekiel were given unspeakable words, "I am broken with their whorish heart which has departed from Me" (Ezek 6:9).

It's the shortest verse in all the Bible: "Jesus wept." Read this book, and you'll take a giant step towards knowing why.

— Winkie Pratney

PREFACE

For the Lord has heard the voice of my weeping.
PSALM 6:8

We have been shocked until we are numb. The images we see on the nightly news and in the morning edition flicker in our tired eyes and weary minds. At one time we would have been grieved to our very core by the atrocities. Now we simply click the remote or turn the page. Enough is enough!

Mankind's continual rejection of impending judgment and his constant spitting in the face of God has all taken its toll.

And now, with a worn-out conscience like a seasoned sinner, we drift into a state of oblivion — unfeeling, untouchable, ignoring accountability. God's church has become undeniably desensitized. And while we purposely lose ourselves, misty-eyed, in the latest best-selling fantasy, true stories of pain, grief and death are being played out in living color next door.

Today, addiction among Christians has hit an all-time high — not to pills and pot but to paper and print. We have become lost in the imaginary and are being held captive without resistance. Like junkies, we come down from our high craving another fix. Just in time —another blockbuster, another illusion! "Take me out of this world!" we shout deep within.

But that will never happen — the Lord won't permit it. And, while reality beckons our response, the danger creeps even closer. Death and destruction are at our doorstep. Pain and misery won't leave us alone. God is forcing us to face up to it all.

Almost everyone agrees, "It's never been like this before." Bad things are happening to good people. Let me rephrase that to be more accurate: Very bad things are happening to very good people.

I think of the words spoken by King Solomon more than three thousand years ago: "Then I looked again at all the acts of oppressions which were being done under the sun. And behold I saw the tears of the oppressed and that they had no one to comfort them; and on the side of their oppressors was power, but they had no one to comfort them" (Eccl. 4:1).

Consider Solomon's heartbreaking statement for just a moment. Does it have a familiar ring? Does it describe the way you feel as you watch the news or scan the headlines? At this very moment innocent victims of war are being raped, beaten and left to die. Young children wail over a pine box as Mommy is lain in the ground forever. Suddenly the grim reality of death settles into your living room —into your soul — like a black cloud. And you realize that in three thousand years nothing has changed.

Like everyone else, I am appalled at the condition of our planet. The events of our day are heart-wrenching: chaotic killings; senseless suffering; deranged derelicts, ventilating with explosives, crushing the innocent in a rage of fury; monthly temper tantrums by tyrants who are fed by their violent passion for more, more, more; gun-toting children marauding neighborhoods, "protecting" their gang's "territorial rights."

Gutters, hospitals and morgues overflow with martyrs to the god of alcohol and drugs. Pressured politicians gasp for breath in a polluted sea of corruption. Government leaders topple like dominos. Food for the hungry is ripped off or rotting. Blatant perversions parade down main street under the guise of "alternative lifestyles." The unborn are massacred meaninglessly. Millions of once God-fearing believers are tossed about by every wind of doctrine. Hatred simmers at a boiling point, just waiting for an excuse to blow. Young people take their own lives, unable to cope with life's daily pressures. The list goes on and on.

The truth of the matter? There exists a very real spirit realm, and we are deceived by a very real enemy. Good and evil are at war. Our hearts are the battleground. Our souls are the spoils of war.

Injustice and turmoil have always existed. From the jealous rage of Cain who murdered his brother Abel, to the demented mind of Adolf Hitler in this century, man has continually bathed himself in blood. The law of the jungle is the law of the asphalt — it's simply survival of the fittest.

Hurt and pain have followed man and will follow him all the days of his life. And an unwanted but constant companion, the prince of darkness, patiently plods alongside him, guiding his every step, deceiving him, stealing from him and slowly destroying him. Satan's success at this should come as no surprise to anyone. After all, his most sought-after possession is the raw material of the human heart — and it is already deceitfully wicked, even before he tampers with it. "The heart is deceitful above all things, and desperately wicked: who can know it?" (Jer. 17:9, KJV).

I can testify personally to Satan's skill as a manipulator. Caught up in his lies at an early age, I was led down the path of destruction. Seeds of deception, perfectly planted throughout my childhood and carefully watered through my adolescence, yielded a garden of healthy but useless weeds. Good was choked out by evil. Soon I was caught in the clutches of rebellion, alcohol and drugs. Jail became my second home.

My heart was hard — I lived in agony. The soil of my soul was war-torn and barren. I wanted out but couldn't find the door.

Indeed, my story was one of total bondage. Yet it ended, like millions of others, with the thrilling experience of deliverance and new life. Jesus Christ came to seek and to save the lost. He found me, mended my wounds and set me on the path of eternal life. And now, having concluded more than two decades as a free man, I write this book.

My purpose in writing it is to answer a question I've had to confront for years in my extensive travels as an evangelist. Christians all over the world know the who, what, when, where and why of evangelism — and yet, we still lament meager success. The question constantly arising is, "How can I be more effective in confrontational evangelism?"

I've worked in several countries, preaching the gospel from city sanctuaries to city slums, and I've come to a few conclusions. Through all the successes and failures, I've learned innumerable lessons.

I've had to sift through thousands of complex problems, to pray with countless hurting individuals. I've witnessed the Lord save the unsaveable, heal the unhealable, love the unlovable.

I've seen mercy poured out on sinners and harsh judgments on the self-righteous. And I've learned that no matter how overwhelming one's situation may seem, there is hope. I have seen "mountains melt like wax in the presence of the Lord" (Ps. 97:5). Despondency dies when God comes on the scene!

After years of seeing the gospel both accepted and rejected, I've finally concluded that, regardless of their outward expression, people are desperately alone. Outwardly, they can be as bold as a lion, but inwardly as gentle as a dove. The hand that throws rocks in adamant rebellion could be attached to a heart that's crying out for something to believe in. A man can come across as being totally together, completely convinced of his happiness and fulfillment but inside be drowning in a sea of confusion. The Word of God so explicitly declares that "even in laughter, the heart may be in pain" (Prov. 14:13).

I've witnessed firsthand many angry, street-hardened gang members weeping tears of repentance as their loneliness was revealed. The masks came floating off in a stream of tears.

I've seen businessmen and women plead for forgiveness, confessing their emptiness, craving a touch from their Creator. I've seen demon-possessed people cry out for deliverance, melting at the mention of Jesus' name. And I've watched in wonder as teenagers, enveloped in the power of God, plead in unison, "What can we do to be saved?"

From the success-driven madman on Wall Street to the shack dweller in Colombia, one common characteristic appears in everyone. It surfaces among the rich and the poor alike, the intellectual and the senseless, the inmate on death row and the sweet grandma next door, the white collar and the blue, the melancholy and the jubilant. There is a common thread — a critical need.

You see, behind all the perplexities, underneath the well-painted facades, past the countless barriers of religious theology, there remains a human soul created by God with a desire to know Him.

Regardless of what a person says or does, he feels a terrible emptiness as long as he lives separated from his Creator. He will never be truly happy until he is spiritually reunited with God.

Hundreds upon hundreds of books have been written on how to move a person from Point A — a godless life driven by selfish desires and ambitions — to Point B — a new creature in Christ Jesus, motivated by love and enjoying continual fellowship with the Creator.

But this book will focus on a missing ingredient that seems to be a vital key in presenting the truth of Christ to unbelievers. Throughout the Scriptures men and women were moved and motivated by this element. And for centuries preachers and evangelists have watched in amazement as something so innocent and tender has produced changes so powerful and effective in people's lives. Evangelists have abused it, and pastors have confused it.

I speak of the language of tears, of weeping before God over our sinful condition and over the lost state of man. This is by no means an exhaustive study on the subject but is rather a compilation of years of research and personal experiences. You'll read detailed accounts of meetings in which the sovereign presence of God produced waves of weeping. You'll travel through the journals and into the hearts and minds of David Brainerd, George Whitefield, Charles Finney, Dwight L. Moody, Evan Roberts, Robert Murray McCheyne and others on whom the presence of God fell, producing sobs and tears of repentance. You'll discover why some people believe they are physically unable to shed tears and what can be done about it. Medical science will show us the physiological makeup of tears — how they're produced and what makes us cry. Do I have dry-eye syndrome, and if so, can I be healed?

We'll weep with the Lord over the present condition of man. We'll take visits to the dry, crusty surface of the heart, where a message drenched in tears can soften the soil, plant the seeds and ripen to a bountiful harvest. Hopefully, we'll come to the truth behind the words of General William Booth, founder of The Salvation Army, who wrote to a frustrated, ineffective group of evangelists: "Try tears! Try tears!"

I pray that by the end of this book, you'll cry out with Jeremiah, "Oh that my head were waters, and mine eyes a fountain of tears, that I might weep day and night for the slain of the daughter of my people!" (Jer. 9:1). And I hope that you'll confess with the psalmist, "My tears have been my meat day and night, while they continually say unto me,

Where is thy God?" (Ps. 42:3, KJV).

We have entered hard times. According to the Holy Scriptures, life as we know it on this earth is only going to get worse. All of creation is groaning for the end. Wickedness is at an all-time high. Evil men and seducers are increasing, and perilous times are upon us, just as Paul predicted (2 Tim. 3).

Many people are hardened but not hopeless. The confused can be calmed. The lost can be found. The hateful can be healed. The Lord assures us, "To every thing there is a season...a time to weep, and a time to laugh; a time to mourn, and a time to dance" (Eccl. 3:1,4, KJV).

This is the time to weep!

ONE

A PERSONAL FAMINE

*We need sincere tears to fall on the parched,
cracked soil of people's hearts,
preparing the way for the life-producing
seed of God's Word.*

Deep conviction and godly fear were on every face in the plaza. Upper-class businessmen and women wept openly. Tears soaked the ground. Across the street a government official left his office, came to the plaza and broke before the Lord.

A teenage member of a cult cried tears of joy as he met his true Savior. High school students pressed in by the scores. They remained for hours — as one person noted, "as if nailed to the pavement." More than two hundred teenagers, many from middle and upper-class backgrounds, were saved that day. One businesswoman received Christ, then ran to get her friends. They too embraced the Lord.

With a conviction I've rarely seen among the wealthy, this woman said, "Don't leave Curico. Please don't leave our city. God is visiting us. You've got to stay!"

Others testified of trying to cross the plaza but were unable to move because something was drawing them. Business appointments were canceled, lunches forgotten and schedules changed, as sinners remained for hours.

There was no hype surrounding the meeting. As soft worship music played over the P.A. system, our team simply flowed through the crowd. Each inquiring sinner was confronted directly about his or her soul.

The result? I've never led so many people to Jesus, one-on-one, during such a short period of time. Tears streamed down our faces. The passage from Scripture was ringing true: "He that goeth forth and weepeth, bearing precious seed, shall doubtless come again with rejoicing, bringing his sheaves with him" (Ps. 126:6, KJV).

We were seeing incredible results that day in the city of Curico, Chile. Indeed the harvest was plentiful, but there was much more to come. I believe it was the direct result of obedience to the Lord.

Let me explain. Not long before, God had brought me through one of the most difficult times of my life. Someone once said, "God can pull you through anything, if you can stand the pull." The showers from heaven I was now experiencing had followed a bitter, dry famine.

Several years ago, at the height of a personal spiritual drought, the Lord began dealing with me intensely about a particular area: tears. I had been laboring faithfully in the harvest fields of Argentina. My devotional life was intact, and my marriage was strong. A whirl of activity was producing some wonderful new churches.

Up to that point, my wife and I had experienced our share of trials and tribulations. We had been the personal recipients of several onslaughts from the enemy. Jeri had suffered numerous physical problems. Some were healed by prayer, others through surgery supported by prayer. During many financial setbacks we fasted and prayed — and we beheld the wonders of the Lord who answered our every need.

We had learned several years earlier that most incredible victories are immediately followed by equally incredible battles. The American evangelist Dwight L. Moody (1837–1899) once said, "The devil is always waiting for you at the foot of the mountain." How true. He often waits patiently, in ambush, for an opportune time.

Many of our victories had been won by a word from the Lord prior to the battle: "Do not fear or be dismayed because of this great multitude, for the battle is not yours but God's. Tomorrow go down against them" (2 Chr. 20:15-16).

Other victories were won by a simple trust in the Lord during the midst of violent warfare. "And they were helped against them, and the Hagrites and all who were with them were given into their hand; for they cried out to God in the battle, and He was entreated for them, because they trusted in Him" (1 Chr. 5:20).

Now we were riding the crest of a wave of great revival in Argentina. That's when the Lord began a deep examination of my heart. During this time of great spiritual exploits, many of our ministry's workers grew disgruntled. The workload was extremely burdensome. They began demanding more money. A spirit of discontentment had settled in the camp. The Lord began cutting off the flow of blessing.

Suddenly attitudes were wrong. Motives were twisted. The work of the ministry had become an occupation — and God had begun some serious sifting. Hard lessons were being taught at an unbelievable rate.

I remembered the saying, "We are all in the school of God — and we never graduate." Now it was examination time. Everyone had been given a pop quiz. We were all being weighed in the balance, and many were found wanting. I myself found the pressures too much to bear. So I began hiding away in my secret place to spend time with the Lord.

My seclusion during the morning hours in those days proved invaluable. Joseph Caryl (1602–1673) once said, "According to the weight of the burden that grieves you is the cry to God that comes from you."[1] My motivation in pursuing Him had been His revelation of the dangers surrounding our exploits. After all, who were we to think that Satan was going to "turn over" thousands of his captives (prisoners of war) without a major conflict? It was time to pursue the Lord like never before. My passionate desire became to see more of God and less of man in our ministry. I wanted a fresh touch, a new anointing. I craved intimacy with Jesus.

Early one morning I flipped open my journal and read a portion I'd written several years earlier. The words became a fresh revelation to my soul:

> I sense a longing in my soul to know Him, the power of His resurrection, the fellowship of His sufferings.
>
> This is such a tender time for Jeri and me. We have been fasting for several days with the intent of drawing close to our Savior. He redeemed us both many years ago, but now He wants us to break into a new dimension of His likeness.
>
> There is such a work to do in this world. I am afraid, not

of man or beast but of self. I know that in my own strength I can hold crusades and build churches. But it mustn't be done in my own strength.

My feelings at that time echoed a thought I later read by the father of the Reformation in the 1600s, Martin Luther. He said: "I am more afraid of my own heart than I am of the pope and all his cardinals. I have within me the great pope — SELF."[2] The writings of Robert Murray McCheyne add the final touch of truth: "There is nothing more deceitful than your estimate of your own strength."[3]

My journal entry continued:

Only the works built from the throne room of God will last. Sometimes my energy can be my worst enemy. My eagerness to work, my fervor for lost souls, my zeal for the work of God, often cloud the true purpose of life.

To live is Christ. My career must be Christ. There is nothing in this world more important than drawing from the well of God's Word; to lie at the feet of Jesus; to be taught, instructed, guided and directed by my Lord and Master.

I long for the entity of Christ. To know Him is to love Him. To know Him is to talk to Him, to listen, to obey.

What a joy it is to sit in His presence and learn of Him. His ways are not our ways. His thoughts are not our thoughts. Might I go further to say His plans, techniques, methods and so forth are not as ours. I must continually immerse myself in the presence of God. From God, and God only, I must receive my instructions for the day.

I feel that the problem is not the workers; it's the depth of their walk that is lacking. The Lord needs workers who are willing to take instructions from the Lord of the harvest. It's so easy, with all of man's wisdom and understanding, to jump into the work of God. We plow, turn, toss the seed, fertilize, water and reap without looking once to the Lord of the harvest.

What is He saying? What is His timing? Where are His fields? Who is He stirring? I must know what is on the heart of my Jesus. I must come daily to His table.

Deep down we all agree with Solomon. On the verge of a great responsibility he confessed, "I am but a little child; I do not know how to go out or come in...give thy servant an understanding heart" (1 Kin. 3:7,9).

So here I was again, several years later, sitting at the Master's feet, craving the crumbs that fell from that heavenly table. Once again I was passing through a dry, spiritual valley. I have grown to appreciate these difficult times. They are not times of doubting God but rather of pursuing Him. "Everything which may be an occasion of grief to the people of God," says John Flavel, "is not a sufficient ground for their questioning the reality of their Christianity. Whatever be the grounds of one's distress, it should drive him to, not from God."[4] Now, the Lord, in His merciful way, began revealing to me His thoughts.

He first led me to the cross — and He gave me time to climb back on. Before going any further, let me explain. We all agree that the Lord's work on the cross was complete. Just as Christ did, I believe we must walk the Calvary road, make our way to Golgotha's hill and pass through the pains and humiliation of crucifixion in order to rise in newness of life. Once we have passed through this experience we can proclaim with the apostle Paul, "I am crucified with Christ: nevertheless I live; yet not I, but Christ liveth in me: and the life which I now live in the flesh I live by the faith of the Son of God, who loved me, and gave Himself for me" (Gal. 2:20, KJV). We are now living dead men. Dead to sin but alive to God. "Likewise reckon ye also yourselves to be dead indeed unto sin, but alive unto God through Jesus Christ our Lord" (Rom. 6:11, KJV).

It's after the resurrection to new life that we begin to hear the approaching hoofbeats of the enemy. Read more about the ensuing warfare in Romans, chapters 6, 7 and 8. We now present our bodies, on a daily basis, as a living sacrifice (Rom. 12:1-2) and die daily to our sinful nature. This is elementary but extremely difficult for most believers.

In the series, *Ministry*, by J. B. Stoney, we find this bold admonition: "I am crucified with Christ. If you fail, you revive the flesh; I have no right to revive the flesh, and if I do revive it and do not judge it, I revive what God has judicially brought to an end in the death of His Son. It is not only that I do a wrong thing, but it is a grievous thing to revive that which God has set aside from His eye."[5]

You see, the only problem with being a "living sacrifice" is the living part; that is, we can crawl on and off the altar at will. Leonard

Ravenhill often said to me, "The only reason you have to get back on the altar today is if you got off yesterday. We should quit singing, 'There's room at the cross for you,' and begin singing, 'There's room on the cross for you.'"

From the cross we gain a whole new perspective. Nailed down, unable to move, sapped of all physical strength and stamina, stripped of all selfish desires and ambitions, we are defenseless. That is where the true man or woman of God learns about trust. In the words of our Master, "Into Thy hands I commit my spirit" (Luke 23:46).

From the cross I began to see lost humanity through the eyes of Christ. Suspended between heaven and earth, eternity becomes clearer. We see the vast separation between God and man. We see lost, starving sheep without a shepherd. Blind men groping in darkness — without hope, destined for destruction.

True compassion comes from a deep understanding of the entire picture. I saw more clearly: He is their only hope. I've learned the lesson before — it's time to learn it again. It's Christ and Christ alone.

From the cross — high enough to get a better view, yet low enough to communicate — we begin to understand the scheme of life. It's a vapor, a mist, a withering flower, a breath. In the eyes of eternity, life is over in seconds.

My personal famine was coming to an end. The longer I hung there, the clearer everything became. As the flesh died, the spirit began to emerge. Paul's statement once again came alive: "I am crucified with Christ: nevertheless I live; yet not I, but Christ liveth in me: and the life that I now live in the flesh I live by the faith of the Son of God, who loved me, and gave himself for me" (Gal. 2:20, KJV).

On the cross a desire for heavenly moisture became intense within me: "I thirst. Dear Lord, I'm so thirsty." From the cross I saw that Jesus had caused the famine. He was leading me through the desert and now was satisfying my craving for living water. "How blessed is the man whose strength is in Thee; in whose heart are the highways to Zion! Passing through the valley of Baca [tears], they make it a spring" (Ps. 84:5-6). "Those who suffer from a scanty supply of water press on through a dry valley, and yet do not despair or grow weary, but have God for their fountain, from which they drink and are refreshed."[6]

The longer I studied Christ, talked to Him, worshiped Him and read about other men's experiences with Him, the clearer everything became. My tears flowed freely as He revealed His only desire for me: To know Him, walk with Him and commune with Him is our whole duty. My talents and abilities were laid waste in the presence of the Lord. Any successes seemed as nothing. Failures faded as well.

I felt the tears cleanse my spiritual eyes. Henry Ward Beecher understood this experience:

> Astronomers have built telescopes which can show myriads of stars unseen before; but when a man looks through a tear in his own eye, that is a lens which opens, reaches into the unknown, and reveals worlds which no telescopes, however skillfully constructed, could do; nay, which brings to view even the throne of God, and pierces the nebulous distance where are those eternal truths in which true life consists.[7]

The tears continued to flow. They flowed for months. Crying out to God with holy tears has a way of cleansing our spiritual eyes. Just as a physical tear washes the physical eye of any disturbing substance, so a heavenly tear cleanses us of spiritual impurities. And how much more so! When it's genuine, we can see better. Jesus was cleansing my spiritual eyes.

During this time of spiritual refreshment, the Word of God became my life-source. What a treasure He has left us in His Word. I also became enthralled with the writings of our spiritual ancestors. I began drinking deeply from the works of George Whitefield, David Brainerd and scores of others. I had read, studied and even given written reports on these revivalists in the past; but now their lives and ministries took on new meanings for me. These men had witnessed something I longed to experience.

Please understand — in my short life as a Christian I had seen more than most people see in a lifetime. After all, I had been marvelously delivered from drugs. I had seen thousands of people come to Jesus, both in the United States and in foreign countries. I had seen lame people walk and blind people receive sight. On scores of occasions I had seen demon-possessed people kick and scream and froth at the mouth, only to succumb under the power of Christ. I had been part of the great Argentina revival, in which hundreds of thousands knelt at the cross. What more could I want? The answer was and still is: plenty.

I longed for something sovereign: no frilly crusade services where people were enchanted by a flashy evangelist; no big attraction where thousands would come to experience something weird or different; no "new" supernatural manifestations that came and went like the wind.

I wanted a deep, holy move of the Spirit. Not among Christians, but among sinners! I wanted to see God come down in a way that would cause everyone to proclaim, "This is the presence of the Lord!"

Little did I know, Jesus was about to open to me a realm of ministry that would surpass everything imaginable. Within a few short months I would begin seeing people melt in the presence of the Lord. Sinners would be drawn, not by some new thing but by the sovereign presence of the Lord.

My personal famine produced an intense desire for the genuine. I wanted to see sinners drawn to the Lord just by sensing His presence. I wanted to feel the hurt, confront the need and see tears of repentance flow. Above all, I wanted to see a deep work, resulting in a life-transforming experience with Jesus Christ.

He answered my prayer. That day at the plaza was an example. Marcia hugged her best friend, Jacqueline, saying she wanted to cry. I said, "Look at me — I'm weeping for you! Go ahead and cry."

A teenage crowd gathered around the two girls. One young man said, "We can feel the presence of God. Now what do we do?" We prayed, and they all received Christ. Marcia burst into tears. That night, in our tent campaign, Jacqueline and Marcia were at the altar with five new friends.

The love and mercy of God that day raced like arrows straight to the heart. The blessed Holy Spirit was drawing hungry hearts to Jesus. A car carrying three spiritually hungry college students and their grandmother stopped. This was their third time back. I got in the car and shared Jesus with them. They had never felt anything like the presence of Christ that was there. Two of the girls broke and sobbed. All four received Christ.

Every day that followed was rich with salvation experiences. The list went on and on. Within a few days, hundreds had embraced their new-found Savior. God had transformed this park of earthly pleasures into a place of heavenly piety. "Rain, Holy Spirit. Rain!"

Since then, the Lord has allowed me to see a spiritual dimension of ministry that goes beyond words. I'd never before seen the hardest of sinners — including rich and poor, cult members, scores of teenagers

— literally trembling in the presence of the Lord. People who hadn't even heard the preaching, who were ignorant of what was taking place, began inquiring about their souls.

The seventeenth-century English pastor Richard Baxter said, "Go to poor sinners with tears in your eyes, that they may see you believe them to be miserable, and that you unfeignedly pity their case. Let them perceive it is the desire of your heart to do them good."

George Whitefield's words reflect what took place in our campaign and those that would follow: "The present work of the Holy Spirit seems to be remarkable and extraordinary, on account of the numbers wrought upon. We never before saw so many brought under soul concern, and with great distress making the inquiry, 'What must we do to be saved?'"[8]

Read on, my friend. Over and over again we have seen the Lord's presence fall like rain on crowds of starving, thirsty people. He transcends denominational barriers, and He desires to visit you.

This book is being published in the midst of a wonderful, refreshing rain from heaven. We are witnessing tremendous manifestations as the Holy Spirit begins to satisfy the hungry heart. Tens of thousands of converted and unconverted souls have been seen moaning and groaning in response to the Spirit of God digging deeply into their hearts. I am so thankful that one of the prominent characteristics of this fresh move of the Holy Spirit is brokenness and tears.

Yes, the Word of the Lord is being preached in a dry, barren wilderness. The struggles of coping with everyday life, the seemingly endless barrage of filth, the lack of spiritual leadership in the pulpit and countless other problems have laid waste the dry hearts of the masses.

But your tears will fall on the parched, cracked soil of people's hearts, preparing the way for the life-producing seed of His Word. The moisture of a heavenly tear is a God-sent shower to the spiritually barren.

Two

FAMINE IN THE LAND

*Humankind is experiencing extreme
spiritual famine — and a starving
humanity will devour anything
that brings personal satisfaction.*

The teenagers approached the car with robbery on their minds. Inside were two weary tourists resting from their long day's journey. The nightmare began.

The young gang jumped up and down on the fenders until the couple inside woke up. Perhaps at first the visitors thought it was just a game. But no one was laughing. Startled and confused, the man in the driver's seat turned on the ignition. *Is this a bad dream,* he wondered, *or are we about to be robbed? We've got to get out of here!*

Then it happened. One of the youngsters pulled out a gun and riddled the rented vehicle with bullets. Utterly shocked, the driver slammed the car into reverse to try to get away. Then the gunplay turned deadly. The weapon was raised. Bullets began to fly.

Within a few moments it was over. "He's dying!" the woman screamed to the 911 operator. "Please help us! My husband is dying!"

"This is the spot," the officer explained.

During our travels, I make it a point to visit areas I consider to be of extreme importance. The pulse of the people is what I'm after. The officer at this rest stop was explaining in detail the events of another tourist killing. Once again, robbery was the motive. And, as in so many others, a gun was flashed and someone had to die.

From riddling the car body to riddling human bodies. After all, what's the big difference?

A highway nap turned into a nightmare. Another desensitized child had expressed only what he'd seen and heard so many times in so many ways. Another chilling episode in the life of America. Murder — it happens every day of every month of every year.

The officer explained several more killings, all occurring over a five-day period. The mode of operation was the same in each: Human beings were treated like sick dogs. Gunned down, knifed or run over for a few bucks. Dead or alive — what's the difference?

Another officer gave me some free advice. "Sir, get a gun. Carry it everywhere you go. These are children with live ammunition. Kill them before they kill you." Great counsel. Everyone packing pistols.

A visit we made to the burned-out streets of south Los Angeles revealed similar attitudes. A friend and I walked the streets of those neighborhoods just after a violent riot had occurred. People had been cut down like animals. The color of your skin, the class of your car, the wrong look — all were legitimate reasons to be assassinated.

People were still simmering. We could feel the intensity. "Hey, man, what are you doing here?" one shouted. "Are you nuts? Don't you know the danger to a white face in this neighborhood?"

Yes, we were aware of the danger. I knew that just around the corner a white truck driver had been beaten senseless and nearly killed. We had just passed miles of burned-out buildings. But we were more curious about the feelings of the people than we were fearful.

Of course, like everyone else, I knew the obvious reasons for the bloodshed. Live video footage had only fueled the fire. But the river of venom here ran much deeper than the news could ever show. All the burned-out buildings depicted burned-out lives. It was a war zone, but why? Why such violence?

Our conversation continued. "You don't hate me, and I don't hate you," I responded. Within a few minutes my friend and I were out-numbered but at total peace. "When you came out of your mama's womb, you didn't have a built-in hatred for whites. You can prove that by mixing kids together in a playpen. They're color-blind. Somebody taught you how to hate." They agreed.

Our talk concluded with my explanation of how Jesus Christ had delivered me from violence and rebellion. I was not a stranger to the streets nor to jail. I agreed with them about the injustices of our day. They were absolutely right — life isn't fair.

"But to end all this violence we need a common denominator. To bring order to this chaos we need a peacemaker, a mediator. Someone who understands both sides. That man is Jesus Christ."

Suddenly their empty lives were being satisfied by truth. They listened intensely and nodded in agreement. As we shook hands, one man said, "Next time you're in this area, my home is your home."

We departed with a gut conviction that Christ is the only answer to the rioting and killing; not gun control but heart control; not weapons but weeping; not violence in the streets but vigilance over our souls.

The coloring of America must be viewed from the cross. "For He Himself is our peace, who made both groups into one, and broke down the barrier of the dividing wall" (Eph. 2:14).

Humankind is experiencing extreme spiritual famine. A starving humanity that craves personal satisfaction will devour anything that has life. The current famine for truth is resulting in severe violence and revolution. Dastardly deeds of darkness are rampant due to the absence of light. Brute force is being used to satisfy inner cravings.

It is a travesty! We see the effects everywhere, but we have to confront the causes. Can something be done? If so, how can we do it? The tragic truth is, America has sown to the wind and is reaping the whirlwind. As prayer went out our back door, perversion came in through the front. As a result, our country is experiencing a mutiny.

Yet while this full-fledged rebellion is taking place, the church is asleep in the captain's cabin. But we can't hide forever. The commotion is critical, and it won't just go away. Government can't legislate this kind of rebellion. Schools can't educate against it. Right now it's banging on the door. Why can't we hear it?

Have you ever noticed how the warfare seems to come in waves? So often the church is lulled to sleep by an apparent slowdown of enemy activity or a sweeping Christian trend, only to be shocked awake by another deadly onslaught. The church must respond now! We must open our eyes, take a closer look and violently confront the powers of darkness.

Shortly after the Los Angeles riots, I found myself at a gay and lesbian march in Washington, D.C. To the participants it was a victorious occasion. To me it was a parade of perpetual pain.

The march served as an indication of just where we are as a nation. Hundreds of thousands of homosexual men and women crowded the Washington Mall to demand equal rights and celebrate their coming out of the closet. The news media wouldn't dare share the truth; what we saw in our homes was shaded. But what I saw in vivid color would shock the nation.

From sadomasochists to state senators, young children to grown men and women, people of all kinds were active participants. Nudity was the rule of the day. Many cursed the established church while toting signs proclaiming, "God is gay."

AIDS hasn't hindered their hellish ambitions — one more lover, a few more pleasures. "Leave us alone!" they cry. "Shame, shame, shame!" they chanted. "Shame on you for trying to deny us our freedom!"

They've crawled out of the closet and into our classrooms. Textbooks have been written in cushy tones, meant to desensitize our little ones — titles include *Daddy's Roommate* and *Heather Has Two Mommies*. "This isn't abnormal behavior," they preach sweetly. "It's just different. So what if Daddy's roommate is his bedmate? Do you have a problem with that?" they scream. And, "Isn't it wonderful that Heather has two mommies!" These books are just the beginning. The presses are standing ready to churn out more diluting discourses.

The march was over and the city was crawling with tourists, mostly homosexuals, from all over the world. I stood at the base of the Lincoln Memorial — at the feet of the man who set captives free. Abraham Lincoln believed in fasting and prayer. He was a man who recognized the depravity of our nation and boldly called us back to God; a man who was not ashamed of the Lord Jesus Christ; a man who would call homosexuality by its real name: sin.

Yet all around me that day were hundreds of slaves. They were bound not with shackles of iron but chains of sin. And they were thanking Lincoln's likeness for their freedom. What an outrage!

Looking up I imagined what Abe would do today. He was a weeper — and I know his tears would drip to the pavement! The anguish of seeing our nation separated from God would grieve him beyond words. I apologized to President Lincoln for allowing our country to slip so far and reconfirmed my allegiance to the cause. I repented for the present famine, the lack of spiritual truth. My words to Abe

Lincoln? "The gospel of Jesus Christ will be preached once again in the streets of America. We will once again pray in our schools. We will fight the fight!"

Where is it all going to end? Wrong is now right, and right is wrong. What was once appalling is now appealing. We are being tormented and tossed. The lack of godly leadership, the confusion of divided homes, the rising tide of evil — all have shipwrecked our society.

I call it perpetual pain — it never ceases. But those aren't the only sources of our pain. What about the torrent of natural disasters?

Earthquakes and hurricanes mercilessly leave in their wakes devastation, destruction and death. Solid family homes are blown away like a house of cards. Towering temples tumble to the ground.

Levees give way to torrential rains, and a peaceful river becomes a sea of grief. A lifetime of work is washed away in an instant, a lifetime of memories buried in a watery grave. Sorrow is added to sorrow.

Meanwhile, as the weather threatens, murder stalks the streets. Highway rest stops become death stops. Passive patrons at restaurants become sitting ducks as angry killers ventilate their frustrations. A car, a fast-food diner, a train, your workplace, now all prime locations for murder. At the neighborhood park, innocent children are preyed upon by lecherous maniacs — kidnapped, sodomized, slaughtered. Even the haven of home has become a living hell for many young lives. We warn them to watch out for strangers outside the home, while their own parents are planning their murder on the inside.

Around the globe are wars and rumors of wars. Thousands of men, women and children are hacked to death during tribal rivalries. Rivers and lakes are contaminated as they become dumping grounds for rotting corpses. What is happening? No one seems to understand why.

Most Christians don't fully comprehend why things are the way the are, but we do see the effects. We realize why the apostle Paul warned us of impending perilous times. Few would deny that we are experiencing God's judgment on earth. We are seeing the natural outcome of "the wages of sin" (Rom. 6:23) — death.

Doesn't it all make you wonder, *Is there a spiritual awakening going on anywhere? Is humanity waking from its sin and slumber?* The answer is yes, there is an incredible awakening! The unsettling of all our securities has caused people to search for certainty. People are looking for a solid foundation, something to stake their lives on. Across this continent and around the world the pursuit is on!

Yet tragically, hungering people are being snared by the lure of tasty lies. Cults are attracting starving pilgrims at an alarming rate. Like sheep lined up for the slaughter, they blindly follow their misguided messiah. "Teach me more, lead me into all truth," they bleat as they follow their masters into fiery destruction.

Christians are continually baffled at how a well-educated, upper-class college student could fall into the hands of these "angels of light." Yet like wolves in sheep's clothing, these evil shepherds slip into our meetings, prey on the flock, choose their next victim and leave with one dangling from their mouths. And we believers stand by, dumbfounded.

There is a battle raging for the souls of men! The battleground is the soil of the heart! For many, their heart's soil is war torn and dry, a barren wilderness. They're in the midst of a famine — a famine for truth.

A shepherd who lived in the desert some twelve miles outside Jerusalem saw something that most men have never been able to understand. More than seven hundred years before the birth of Christ, this man saw clearly what is happening today:

> "Behold, days are coming," declares the Lord God, "when I will send a famine on the land, not a famine for bread or a thirst for water, but rather for hearing the words of the Lord. And people will stagger from sea to sea, and from the north even to the east; they will go to and fro to seek the word of the Lord, but they will not find it" (Amos 8:11-12).

Amos saw the sickness of sin. He saw how man made himself the measure of all things, leaving God out of the picture. He saw humanism. He saw that political systems — whether communistic, dictatorial, or democratic — were doomed to fail because of one fatal flaw: They did not recognize the sinful, self-centered nature of man. They ignored God and glorified man.

Amos saw a famine. A famine brought on by God and fueled by man. He saw the spiritual desperation of the world. People were literally starving to death.

The scientific name for the sickness Amos saw is marasmus: the wasting away of the body due to malnutrition. Bloated stomachs and withered limbs characterize this deadly condition.

Amos saw men stumbling on toothpick legs. Young men swallowed dust, fainting to the parched ground from lack of water. Mothers cradled their children who were being eaten with disease — one having just died, another on the verge.

Reality gripped Amos' heart as the picture unfolded. These people were dying from the lack of truth! They craved the Word of the Lord, and it was nowhere to be found.

Famine, by definition, is "an extreme and protracted shortage of food." It is so severe a shortage that it results in widespread starvation, death and a scarcity of anything that can help. Let's take a look at the causes and effects of physical famine. Then we'll draw the spiritual parallels.

Drought, or prolonged lack of rain, has produced widespread famine throughout the world. The great famine in Egypt, A.D. 1064 through 1072, was due to the lack of rain. Crops failed and pasturelands withered. The atrocities that occurred during this famine are hard to believe. Starvation was so widespread that history records barbarians hovering on housetops with ropes and hooks waiting for their prey. When someone walked by, the rope was thrown down, the hook punctured his flesh, and he was hoisted to the roof. Then he was roasted and eaten like an animal.

In the 1870s more than five million people in India perished due to the lack of water. During the same period, more than nine million in China died of famine due to the lack of rainfall.

The United States has had its share of severe droughts. Most of us remember when, in the 1980s, the Midwest, the northern Great Plains and parts of the Southeast were devastated by lack of rain. Our country experienced serious damage to our grain crops. And what about the wildfires? The dry conditions set the stage for an impending disaster. "Out of control!" screams the weary firefighter as the blaze incinerates everything in its path.

We all know that since the 1960s millions of Africans have died of malnutrition brought on by drought. We've seen the pictures: malnourished children crawling across cracked, sun-dried ground; young and old alike, sapped of strength, unable to swat off the flies, waiting to die. Marasmus marauded their homes and villages. And the slaughter continues today.

Spiritually speaking, we have experienced similar heartache, an inner drought. Sin has dried up the hearts of the masses. It saps the very life out of us. Our lack of clean, spiritual water is directly related to deaths and destruction in our world today such as the increasing intensity of the violence among our youth. Wasting away in the desert, they drink from any watering hole, and the result is often fatal. Poisoned water leads to poisoned lives.

And wildfires abound. The winds of darkness blow across their dry, parched lives, whipping the flames into a ferocious inferno. In search of something that satisfies, the youth give in to the heat of peer pressure. Disaster spreads as the fire consumes another precious life.

Science tells us a person can only live about three days without water. If he lies immobile the duration increases to about twelve days. The fact is, we are doomed without water, whether physical or spiritual.

The Bible answers this famine. Jesus said, "He who believes in Me shall never thirst" (John 6:35). He also said, "The water that I shall give him shall become in him a well of water springing up to eternal life" (John 4:14).

The spiritual drought today is obvious. Thirsting souls constantly search for clean, pure water — that which quenches and doesn't curse. Water that flows from clean vessels, not contaminated containers. How many new Christians have withered and died after drinking poisoned water from old, rusty pipes? Preachers and teachers with unclean hearts spit out yellow, tainted messages, leaving bitter aftereffects in the hearts of newborn believers. They have single-handedly polluted the stream of truth. The following advice from Charles Mackintosh needs to be heeded: "The pure water should be allowed to flow from the heart of God to the heart of the sinner, without receiving a tinge from the channel through which it flows."

Another cause of severe famine is too much rainfall and flooding. Rivers swollen by heavy rains overflow their banks and destroy farmland. Other crops rot in the fields because of an excess of water. In the 1300s, several years of heavy rains created widespread famine in Western Europe. In 1929, more than two million people died in China due to flooding. Too much rain caused massive crop failure.

The results? Cats, dogs, rats, rodents and insects were eaten without remorse. In Egypt, the swelling of the Nile River just a few feet can devastate that country's food supply. Around A.D. 1199, a famine there caused incredible tragedy. Human flesh became a very common source of food. Parents consumed their children. Recipes were shared on how to prepare their flesh. During the height of this famine, people resorted to eating those who had died from malnutrition.

During the great Russian famine of this century, the starving masses resorted to eating animal dung. They rejoiced at finding undigested, whole kernels of grain.

Now, what about the church? We've definitely had too much rain, not dew from heaven but acid rain, contaminating every heart it hits. We're being flooded with godless men and women preaching tainted messages to a gullible people. These false prophets and teachers have discovered the ever-increasing market. People are starving for something to believe in. They are famished for food. Truth is what they want, but trash is what they get.

The Bible gives similar accounts of severe famines and their consequences. Second Kings 6 records a famine in Samaria during which a woman killed and ate another woman's son due to severe starvation. In Genesis 25, Esau sells his birthright to Jacob because he's famished. When people are starving, they'll do things that normally would be beyond consideration.

Likewise today, in a spiritual sense, multitudes have ended up eating rats and rodents. Owing to the lack of godliness in the pulpit, many Christians have resorted to eating tough, hard-to-digest spiritual food that offers little or no nourishment. Spiritual disease is rampant. Unclean food has resulted in widespread dysentery in the church body. Once God-fearing believers now lie bedridden and disabled due to improper nourishment.

The famine for truth in our country has hit, and it has hit hard. People are resorting to anything for nourishment. Like a heavy downpour, death-serving cults continue to flood our nation. Like vultures, they hover over the spiritually malnourished. These groups are growing, due partly to the lack of strong, God-ordained leadership in our churches. A good friend of mine spent three years searching for truth in a cultic college before coming to the conclusion it was all heresy. Another Bible college graduate, searching for more truth, became entangled with a group of dissident deceivers. She was brainwashed beyond belief, and we wept for her return. It took months for us to convince her of the cult's deadly errors. In my mission work it is heart-breaking to see how the spiritually destitute will give themselves to false teaching. The spiritually starving masses grasp at anything to eat.

The list of famine causes continue. Swarming insects have played a major part in vast, destructive famines. The locust, or grasshopper, is a migratory insect that has caused unspeakable damage to crops, producing widespread famine. Joel speaks of four means of devastation by locusts: gnawing, swarming, creeping and stripping. Each one picks up where the other leaves off. The result is total destruction.

Many a preacher has used this analogy from the book of Joel to explain the results of habitual sin. It chews away at our lives, and the end result is famine. Spiritual decay leaves us devastated.

King Solomon reminds us of the little foxes that spoil the vine. They nibble and gnaw at the tender shoots. They swallow the grapes. They chew at the bark, and the death of the vine follows. Famine results.

Armies have deliberately created famines to starve their enemies into surrender. They destroy stored food and growing crops and set up a blockade to cut off the enemy food supplies.

Ever heard of a spiritual grain embargo? Satan and his marauding band of cutthroats set up blockades in the hearts and minds of the spiritually hungry. He erects walls of bitterness, hatred, doubts, fears, all blocking the flow of food.

Lack of transportation also has played a major role in the starvation of millions. Often the culprit is not a lack of food but shoddy delivery. The much-needed containers never arrive on time.

The church is guilty in this sense, too. Our storehouse is full — we overflow with blessings. But we're like tractor-trailer rigs, loaded down with enough to feed the world yet without a driver. While the grain rots, we spend our time fighting over who gets to drive, or who gets their name on the side of the truck, arguing over who's going to get the credit for helping. We fight and bicker over whether or not "they want our help." We reason, "If they're so hungry, why not put up a sign? They can come to us." Poor transportation! In the end, mule-drawn trains finally provide food for the hungry while we worship in palaces of gold. What is the answer? What can we do?

First we must seek the presence of the Lord as David did. "Now there was a famine in the days of David for three years, year after year; and David sought the presence of the Lord" (2 Sam. 21:1). Remember, the Word of God boldly declares that the Lord is sending the famine (Amos 8:11). Shouldn't we go straight to the source rather than squabble with side issues? The One sending the famine will instruct us on what to do in the famine. We will be reminded of His many promises: "O fear the Lord, ye His saints: for there is no want to them that fear Him. The young lions do lack, and suffer hunger: but they that seek the Lord shall not want any good thing" (Ps. 34:9-10, KJV). "Behold, the eye of the Lord is upon them that fear Him, upon them that hope in His mercy; to deliver their soul from death, and to keep them alive in famine" (Ps. 33:18-19, KJV). "When the poor and the needy seek water, and there is none, and their tongue faileth for thirst, I the Lord will hear them, I the God of Israel will not forsake them" (Is. 41:17, KJV).

Second we should pray the prayer of Solomon:

> When the heavens are shut up and there is no rain, because they have sinned against Thee, and they pray toward this place and confess Thy name and turn from their sin when Thou dost afflict them, then hear Thou in heaven and forgive the sin of Thy servants and of Thy people Israel, indeed, teach them the good way in which they should walk. And send rain on Thy land, which Thou has given Thy people for an inheritance.
>
> If there is famine in the land, if there is pestilence, if there is blight or mildew, locust or grasshopper, if their enemy besieges them in the land of their cities, whatever plague, whatever sickness there is, whatever prayer or supplication is made by any man or by all Thy people Israel, each knowing the affliction of his own heart, and spreading his hands toward this house; then hear Thou in heaven Thy dwelling place, and forgive and act and render to each according to all his ways, whose heart Thou knowest, for Thou alone dost know the hearts of all the sons of men, that they may fear Thee all the days that they live in the land which Thou has given to our fathers (1 Kin. 8:35-40).

Our first and most important mode of action should be the purification of our hearts. We need a cleansing, a purification. How can we possibly offer a starving world decent food if our own serving hands are filthy?

Like the ancient Samaritans, the church today has become cannibalistic. We eat our own, chewing each other up over petty problems and doctrinal differences. Jesus said it well: "Why beholdest thou the mote that is in thy brother's eye, but considerest not the beam that is in thine own eye?" (Matt. 7:3, KJV). Let's scream at the beam, not gloat over the mote!

Not long ago I received a phone call from a newspaper editor asking about denominational barriers. "People are dying on our doorsteps, and we're bickering over whether they should be sprinkled or immersed," was my statement. "People are starving for truth, knocking on our doors, but their cries are muffled by our constant murmuring."

In many cases such churches have been reduced to rubble. What were once thriving congregations now consist only of dead men's bones. Paul warns, "But if you bite and devour one another, take care lest you be consumed by one another" (Gal. 5:15).

Third we must preach the Word, the Truth, which is Christ. Jesus said, "I am the bread of life; he who comes to Me shall not hunger, and he who believes in Me shall never thirst" (John 6:35). Nothing fills the heart of an unbeliever like the pure Word of God. Yet, take caution: When feeding the hungry, don't overdo it. A spiritually starving soul cannot eat chunks of meat, only tender morsels that are well-prepared. You don't shove a steak down a starving man's throat; you spoon-feed him to health. And when you do this, salt the food with your tears.

The spiritually thirsty need water. Clean water, not carbonated. We have served the starving everything from gin and tonic to soda pop. The masses are either drunk or malnourished. They always come back for more, never satisfied, because what they're receiving is not living water, not the truth. "Always learning and never able to come to the knowledge of the truth," states 2 Timothy 3:7. The crystal rivers of living waters flow only from the uncontaminated springs of the heart.

Let your tears be a source of nourishment. Let them fall on the barren soil. A tear dripping from the eye of a godly man can moisten the soil of a sinner's heart.

Jacob sent his sons to Egypt in search of nourishing food, and God prepared the way. "And the people of all the earth came to Egypt to buy grain from Joseph, because the famine was severe in all the earth" (Gen. 41:57). Today multitudes are staggering from place to place, searching for just a morsel of spiritual food. And God once again has prepared the way. Under the able direction of Joseph, there was plenty. And today, under the leadership of Jesus Christ, there is bread and water to satisfy the craving heart.

Let's honestly ask ourselves: Why are they famished when they can be feasting? Why are they dry when they can be drinking?

THREE

THE SORROW OF THE LORD

*Who grieves with God over the death of
His children? What causes Him grief, and
how can we turn His mourning into dancing?*

J oseph Parker pastored for thirty-three years at the City Temple in London during the late 1800s. He once said, "All the sermons that have ever been preached are reducible to a few pages of written matter. The preacher really has nothing to say except that God wishes that men would return to Him. And that men having returned to Him will be cultivated and strengthened in all righteousness."

This must be why the prophet Micah said, "He has told you, O man, what is good; and what does the Lord require of you but to do justice, to love kindness, and to walk humbly with your God?" (Mic. 6:8).

Solomon came to a similar conclusion: "When all has been heard...fear God and keep His commandments, because this applies to every person. For God will bring every act to judgment, everything which is hidden, whether it is good or evil" (Eccl. 12:13-14).

And, of course, Jesus summed up all of the law and the prophets when He stated, "'You shall love the Lord your God with all your heart, and with all your soul, and with all your mind.' This is the great and foremost commandment. The second is like it, 'You shall love your neighbor as yourself.' On these two commandments depend the whole Law and the Prophets" (Matt. 22:37-40).

Throughout this book you will discover a common thread. What we are learning has been learned by those who have gone before us, and it will be learned by those who follow. In other words, the teaching is eternal because its truth is forever.

The problem emerges when we have been taught over and over again but never live the teaching. When will all this learning take root and grow and bear fruit? When will the Word begin living in our lives? When will its teaching become habitual? We seem to be "always learning and never able to come to the knowledge of the truth" (2 Tim. 3:7). It has been said that in order to form a new habit you must repeat that particular function at least twenty times consecutively. As an example, if you want to wake up earlier you must set your alarm at the desired time, get up when it rings and begin your day for at least twenty times before your body and mind adjust to this new rhythm of living.

This truth was clearly put forth by Thomas à Kempis more than five hundred years ago when he said, "Habit overcomes habit."[1] Sadly, very few of us are willing to pay that kind of price to change some of our governing practices.

If this is true of the physical realm, how much more must the spiritual man be immersed in a teaching again and again until the truth takes hold in him? It must be why Jesus, after spending untold hours teaching His disciples, ventilated His frustration by saying, "O unbelieving and perverted generation, how long shall I be with you? How long shall I put up with you?" (Matt. 17:17). When were they going to begin truly learning? When were they going to live out in their public lives what they learned in their Master's many hours of teaching in private?

I am convinced that many of us are approaching the point of no return. A radical change must take place in our lives, or we are destined to die spiritually. Millions are at this point right now. We have heard but have not listened. We have been taught over and over the eternal value of prayer and fasting, yet still we remain unchanged. We have simmered in evangelism seminars on the love and the mercy of God, yet still we are not winning others. We know the effectiveness of prayer, yet we turn to it as a last resort. We know the Word of God holds the answer to every circumstance and need in our lives, yet still we trust in men and ourselves.

Our heavenly Father has attempted again and again to instruct us in the way we should go. Listen to how the writer of Proverbs explains it:

> Hear, O sons, the instruction of a father,
> And give attention that you may gain [know] understanding,
> For I give you sound teaching;
> Do not abandon my instruction.
> When I was a son to my father,
> Tender and the only son in the sight of my mother,
> Then he taught me and said to me,
> "Let your heart hold fast my words;
> Keep my commandments and live" (Prov. 4:1–4).

Throughout the Word we are patiently instructed by our heavenly Father. The writer of Proverbs also explains that "a foolish son is a grief to his father, and bitterness to her who bore him" (Prov. 17:25). The stark reality of this foolishness is brought home in another heartbreaking verse. "A man who wanders from the way of understanding will rest [literally settle down and remain] in the assembly [congregation] of the dead" (Prov. 21:16). This should come as a welcome slap to the face to the slipping saint. My friend, the endless drifting must stop.

I trust these Scriptures move us safely to the harbor of understanding. We have an accountability with God which we can no longer neglect. Our relationship with Him cannot be one-sided. Yet we have become renegades in this relationship. We've read about the Father-heart of God and how He longs for our fellowship, but we can't seem to find the time for Him. We pay more homage to our home than to heaven. We've mastered recycling and have failed at regeneration. We devote more energy to sports than to the Spirit; more attention to our gifts than to the Giver; more time to our talents than to the Teacher. I don't believe there is a single reader who would disagree: It's time for all believers to get hold of God!

One particular portion of Scripture in the Old Testament has had a profound effect on my life. Most of us have read it time after time, paying little attention to its depth. This passage has to do with the deep feelings of God at this present moment.

We are all so concerned about ourselves, but do we ever wonder what the Lord is going through? Have we ever paused long enough to hear His moanings? Have we spent time listening to His heart's cry?

Right now I want to ask something of you. I'd like for you to read the remainder of this chapter as if the Lord were seated beside you with His arm around you. Now stop for a moment and consider this passage:

> And God saw that the wickedness of man was great in the earth, and that every imagination of the thoughts of his heart was only evil continually. And it repented the Lord that he had made man on the earth, and it grieved him at his heart (Gen. 6:5-6, KJV).

That was the King James Version. The New American Standard reads this way: "And the Lord was sorry that He had made man on the earth, and He was grieved in His heart" ("and His heart was filled with pain," NIV).

This passage is tied directly to one in the New Testament: "But as the days of Noah were, so shall also the coming of the Son of man be" (Matt. 24:37, KJV). All our preaching and teaching pertaining to this passage has to do with the wickedness of our times and the suddenness of the Lord's return. But what of the One who is Lord over it all? What about the One who was holding back the floodgates? What was (and is) He feeling?

We know how bad man had become — and still is — but what about the One who placed him here? All like sheep had gone astray, but what about the Shepherd? All creation was cursing and complaining, but what was the Creator feeling?

Many may remember the cheerful, classic chorus "He's Got the Whole World in His Hands." Well if we believe that He does, then what do we believe He is going to do with it?

We sing this melody with joyfulness of heart, claiming His awesome protection. But is God listening with the same overwhelming joy? Look at what He did back in Noah's day when He had the whole world in His hands!

I've heard many parents jokingly say to their disobedient children, "I brought you into this world, and I can take you out." Well God brought man into this world, and He can take him out at any moment! But what made Him wait during the days of Noah, and why is He waiting now?

During Noah's time, man had broken God's heart to such an extent that God was in deep distress. Man had become rich in creature comforts but destitute in godly character. Man had died spiritually, and God was broken over it. Many of the great theologians agree that the divine "grief" spoken of in verse 6 was the deepest form of sorrow. The actual word is *nacham,* meaning, "to breathe strongly; to comfort oneself in deep sorrow." God's grief was to such a degree that it is implied He had trouble catching His breath. He was bewailing the spiritual death and eternal separation of man, His friend and creation.

Francis Parkman wrote more than a century ago, "When a friend is taken away, we feel that to us chiefly he dieth. There is a vacancy in our hearts, which we know not how to fill. We look around, but we can discern nothing capable or worthy to occupy that sacred place. Every thing human and earthly appears to us inadequate, disproportionate and inferior."[2]

Throughout the centuries, man has handled deep sorrow as best he could. The Hebrews had their own customs for handling deep grief. During times of mourning, a fast was proclaimed, sackcloth was worn and mourners often lay themselves on the ground. During violent outbursts of sorrow, in the instantaneous overflow of lamentation, they wrung their hands above the head or beat their breast. Deep mourners were known even to tear out their beard and hair.[3]

Mourning usually lasted seven days. Oftentimes, wealthy persons hired professional mourning women who uttered loud, wailing cries in the house and at the grave during the days of mourning. Many of these customs are still carried on in several countries to this day.[4]

How does God handle grief and sorrow? Man had died spiritually, and the Giver of life was bemoaning his departure. Who grieves with God over the death of His children?

God had tasted sweet fellowship with His creation. He cherished the company of men such as Enoch: "And Enoch walked with God; and he was not, for God took him" (Gen. 5:24). But God cursed the corruption of men like Cain. "And He [God] said, 'What have you done? The voice of your brother's blood is crying to Me from the ground. And now you are cursed from the ground, which has opened its mouth to receive your brother's blood from your hand'" (Gen. 4:10-11).

Such was the sorrow of the Lord. There was no consolation to be found. All the beasts of the field and the birds of the air couldn't quench the pain of the loss of His beloved friend.

As man began to multiply on the face of the earth, so multiplied his wickedness. Something had to be done during the days of Noah. God said, "My Spirit shall not strive with man forever" (Gen. 6:3). Indeed, something will be done as well today. For every action there will be a reaction. Thomas Adams, a pious English preacher of the 1600s, said aptly, "That which a man spits against Heaven shall fall back on his own face."[5] Man's spit-droplets on earth had created a thundercloud in heaven.

I challenge you to spend time in trying to understand this form of grief. One way to do this might be to question your local funeral home director. Ask him to explain the worst pain and heartache he's ever seen. Perhaps he will tell you of a mother who lost her young child suddenly in a bicycle accident. She remained in shock for hours. The deepest grief known to mankind swept over her like billows of the sea. She gripped the casket and stared at the corpse, letting out moans and groans of sorrow. Finally she leaned over, placing a kiss on her young one's cold, lifeless cheek, soaking his little face with her tears.

Her pain would be beyond words. No human consolation could touch it. At times her agonizing cries would fill the parlor. She would buckle over, weeping and wailing, often losing her breath. Such pain is deep; the sorrow is overwhelming. And her cries often would so affect others that they would enter into her grief and begin to share in her sorrow.

Now perhaps we are beginning to understand the pain God was experiencing (and experiences now) over the loss of His beloved children. He is torn in two. His heart is broken. The very ones who were created to bring Him joy are causing Him deep sorrow.

Remember you have invited the Lord to sit next to us as you read. Now pause for a moment. Look into the eyes of Jesus. Tell me, is He weeping today as He did over Jerusalem?

Put your arm around Him. Console the King. Wait upon Him as you would someone engulfed in human grief. Sometimes the best thing we can do is just to sit still — to simply be there, willing and waiting to serve His every need.

Now let's do something unconventional. Let's make this even more personal by going one step further and placing our name within this text. It would read something like this:

"And God saw that the wickedness of Steve was great in the earth, and that every imagination of the thoughts of Steve's heart was only evil continually. And it repented the Lord that He had made Steve on the earth, and it grieved Him at His heart."

The Word continues: "And I will blot out Steve whom I have created from the face of the land, from man to animals, to creeping things and to birds of the sky; for I am sorry that I have made them."

My friend, this is where we all should begin. As Christians we should never presume that everything is just fine. As the apostle Paul said to the church of Corinth, we should constantly be examining ourselves to see if we are actually in the faith (2 Cor. 13:5). Ask yourself the following questions:

- Is it possible I am in disobedience to the Lord?
- Could there be something in my life that is grieving God?
- Are my actions pleasing to the Lord, or am I causing Him sorrow?
- Is God pleased that He brought me into this world, or is He heartbroken over my life?
- Is there more to have of Him after my initial salvation experience? Is God expecting anything on my part?

Now, for just a few moments, slip out of your position beside the Lord and fall before Him. Bathe His feet with your tears. Join the disciples as they each responded to the Lord's statement, "One of you will betray Me." "Lord, is it I?" they cried. "Surely not me, Master. Lord, is it possible that I am causing You pain and sorrow?"

Acknowledge the distance between you and the Lord. And begin to close the gap with your tears.

> Drop, drop, slow tears,
> And bathe those beauteous feet,
> Which brought from heaven
> The news and Prince of peace.
> Cease not, wet eyes,
> His mercies to entreat;
> To cry for vengeance
> Sin doth never cease.

In your deep floods
Drown all my faults and fears;
Nor let His eye
See sin, but through my tears.[6]

"There is a godly sorrow," said the sixteenth-century Scottish preacher John Welch, "which leads a man to life. This sorrow is wrought in a man by the Spirit of God, and in the heart of the godly, that he mourns for sin because it has displeased God, who is so dear and so sweet a Father to him."

HOW WE GRIEVE THE LORD

The remainder of this chapter will cover some of the areas that bring grief to our Lord. By no means are we going to cover everything that grieves the Lord. A detailed, exhaustive list would demand another book. But we'll touch on several areas that stand out in the Word of God.

At the conclusion we will rejoice over one of the most promising passages of Scripture in the Word of God: "But Noah found favor in the eyes of the Lord" (Gen. 6:8). Those two words — "But Noah" — are as two halogen lights blazing in the darkness. They speak hope to anyone who has wandered from the way of understanding. They are words of resurrection to the dead.

We will conclude by filling in our name for Noah's. "But Steve found favor in the eyes of the Lord." We will examine three characteristics of Noah and seek to incorporate them into our lives. But before we can do that, we must look at several areas that grieve the Lord:

1. WE GRIEVE HIM BY NOT KNOWING HIS WAYS AND BY NEGLECTING HIS GREAT WORK OF ATONEMENT.

The children of Israel grieved the Lord in the wilderness. "Forty years long was I grieved with this generation, and said, It is a people that do err in their heart, and they have not known my ways" (Ps. 95:10, KJV). He had provided for their every need, but it was never enough in their eyes. They always wanted more!

Now thousands of years later we are still grieving the Lord by not knowing His ways. Once again He has provided for our every need, but we still miss Him!

Atonement means making amends; it signifies a bringing together of those who are separated. This was the work of God's sacrificial Lamb. He gave His very best that we might have life. And His work is complete. Jesus' cry, "It is finished," was an all-inclusive declaration, encompassing everything that needed to be done for man's pardon. "Behold the Lamb of God, which taketh away the sin of the world" (John 1:29, KJV). Jesus is the way. We need not add anything to Him nor take away anything from Him. To do so is to grieve Him. All we need is to know Him.

God came down to man. He took upon Himself every pain, every wilderness mile, every sorrow, every rejection. He's provided it all. "He was in violent pain in the garden and on the cross; ineffable was the sorrow that He felt, being forsaken of His Father, deserted by His disciples, affronted and reproached by His enemies, and under a curse for us" (Timothy Rogers, England, 1660–1729).[7]

Everything evil that you and I could possibly suffer during our lifetime, Jesus suffered in a few short years. "For we have not a high priest which cannot be touched with the feeling of our infirmities; but was in all points tempted like as we are, yet without sin" (Heb. 4:15, KJV).

Yet Jesus suffered through this worldly wilderness without a complaint and without a murmur. Listen to the words of Joseph Hall:

> What is this that I see? My Savior in agony, and an angel strengthening Him. Oh the wonderful dispensation of the Almighty! That the eternal Son of God, who promised to send the Comforter to His followers, should need comfort! That He of whom the voice from heaven said, This is my beloved Son, in whom I am well pleased, should be struggling with His Father's wrath even to blood! That the Lord of Life should, in a languishing horror, say, "My soul is exceeding sorrowful, even unto death!" (Matt. 26:38). These, O Savior, are the chastisements of our peace; which both Thou wouldest suffer and Thy Father would inflict. The least touch of one of those pangs would have been no less than a hell to me.[8]

How can we neglect so great a salvation? How can we slight such suffering? His work of redemption is complete. We must preach total atonement!

My thoughts return to an incredible evangelistic campaign where a large group of unconverted young people had gathered. I was well into my message when the Lord struck me with a divine revelation. For twenty minutes I had been sharing stories of powerful conversions. Hoping to attract the listeners' attention, I told of seeing a Hell's Angels' biker weep at the cross, of witnessing scores of teenagers melt in the presence of the Lord, of watching demon-possessed people scream out in agony as Jesus was preached. Yet the more stories I told, the more distant these young unconverted souls became. They began chuckling and cutting up. Several began mocking the message.

Then God spoke to me: "Preach the blood, Steve. If I be lifted up, I will draw all men unto Me. Speak of My suffering, My pain, the Cross."

I was grieving the Holy Spirit. I repented then and there for having missed God, and I quickly got in line with His message and plan. Within just a few minutes, my listeners were weeping uncontrollably. The more I preached the cross, the more they cried. The altars overflowed. My quaint little stories hadn't satisfied. His sacrifice set them free!

Don't bypass the blood or cut out the cross to keep the crowd. His work of atonement is complete!

2. WE CAUSE THE LORD SORROW BY OUR DISOBEDIENCE.

"It is not enough to confess freely and openly our many offenses. Embedded in God's word of forgiveness to us is the call to obedience."[9]

How many times does Jesus have to ask something of us before we do it? Can you imagine if you were the Father and your child were doing some of the things you're doing? How long would you put up with it? How many times would you permit your child to disobey you before you inflicted discipline? Most of us would agree: not long! Our wrath would come down quickly!

My little boy, Ryan, once cried out before he got a well-deserved spanking, "I love you, Daddy! I love you, Daddy!" My reply was simply, "Ryan, if you love me, then obey me!"

The apostle John wrote, "This is love, that we walk according to His commandments" (2 John 6). Be obedient to that still, small voice! Watchman Nee once said that if we care for God's cares, God will take care of our cares.[10] Indeed, obedience is better than sacrifice. "Behold, to obey is better than sacrifice, and to heed than the fat of rams" (1 Sam. 15:22). It's much easier to offer up ritualistic emblems than to obey the voice of the Lord. We soothe our conscience by offering Him our service rather than our lives.

I'll never forget a man in one service who threw his arms around me, sobbing out of control. I was visiting his church and had opened up the altars for those who wanted to pray.

"God called me to the mission field when I was sixteen," he confessed, wiping his eyes. He obviously was broken over his confession. "I made excuses and didn't pursue His call. Over the years I've built a successful business and made plenty of money. I've missed God for the last forty-five years. I've been in the church, served as a deacon, paid my tithes, but I've missed God all these years!"

What a sad, pitiful and unnecessary situation. He'd been out of God's will for over four decades! My counsel to him was to repent and begin to involve himself in every missions project possible. "Don't just confess your failure," I said, "show God how serious you are about changing!" I told him of a couple in our Costa Rican language school who were learning Spanish at age sixty-five. They were on their way to the mission field. It's never too late to begin walking in obedience!

To obey is better than sacrifice. God doesn't want acts of contrition from us, rather He desires a life of obedience.

3. WE CAUSE THE LORD SORROW BY DENYING HIS PRESENCE.

We deny God's presence by our everyday actions. Where has our godly fear gone? "Can any hide himself in secret places that I shall not see him? saith the Lord. Do not I fill heaven and earth? saith the Lord" (Jer. 23:24, KJV).

Why do we hide from His presence? Because like Adam and Eve we try to cover up our wrongdoings. We seek a place in the forest to hide. "And they heard the sound of the Lord God walking in the garden in the cool of the day, and the man and his wife hid themselves from the presence of the Lord God among the trees of the garden" (Gen. 3:8).

What foolishness! Playing hide-and-go-seek with God is a no-win situation. God can see through trees! Besides, hasn't nature taught of the danger of hiding under trees when a storm is brewing? Lightning strikes! Be transparent with the Lord; confess your faults. Repent. Ask His forgiveness. Don't run and hide!

Listen to the words of Isaiah: "I will destine you for the sword, and all of you shall bow down to the slaughter. Because I called, but you did not answer; I spoke, but you did not hear. And you did evil in My sight, and chose that in which I did not delight" (Is. 65:12).

Most of us pretend to believe God is present everywhere, and yet we live as if He were present nowhere. This is a high aggravation of sin. To break a king's laws in his sight is more bold than to violate them behind his back. Yet, this is exactly what we do!

Upon the stark realization of our sin we should cry out with David, "Against Thee, Thee only, I have sinned, and done what is evil in Thy sight" (Ps. 51:4).

> I observed not Thy presence, I neglected Thee while Thy eye was upon me. And this consideration should sting our hearts in all our confessions of our crimes. Men will be afraid of the presence of others, whatsoever they think in their heart. How unworthily do we deal with God in not giving Him so much as an eye-service, which we do man![11]

Determine now to be a pleasing child. Embrace the Father rather than deny His presence. Just as Adam and Eve were forced to confess, sooner or later all of us will stand before Him. Why not now, willingly, rather than later, huddled in a forest of fear?

We should learn from David's deeds. When we've done wrong, we need to face up to it. I think of the words of the English minister Abraham Wright (1611–1690): "We may feel God's hand as a Father upon us when He strikes us as well as when He strokes us."[12] He's our Father. He corrects us because He loves us. He has eternity in mind.

4. WE CAUSE THE LORD SORROW BY HAVING IDOLS IN OUR LIVES.

An idol is anything that sets itself up before God in our lives. The Scriptures are clear: Idolatry is sin and brings severe consequences!

The idol of pride — of being somebody, of desiring a name above other names — has desolated America. Pride, by definition, is "a conceited sense of one's superiority." It is man reveling in all his pomp and power.

Someone said that if Satan can't keep you at the bottom of the ladder he'll help you climb to the top and then push you over. How many great church leaders have risen to the top and been pushed over? Christian socialites act as if there exists a "heavenly sidewalk of stars" where others will come and worship their footprints. Surely, they have their reward: idolatry. But the Lord won't permit it. There is only one star, the Morning Star! Read how harshly Stephen Charnock attacked idolatry:

> To steal away the honor due to God and appropriate it to that which is no work of His hands, to that which is loathsome in His sight, hath disturbed His rest and wrung out His just breath to kindle a hell for its eternal lodging, a God-dishonoring and soul-murdering lust, is worse than to prefer Barabbas before Christ.[13]

Remember, God always sees the heart. A good self-examination of our prideful attitude is always in order. We must see ourselves as God sees us. For example, if every thought that came to your mind over the last week was suddenly projected on a large screen for all to see, what would be the reaction? In total humiliation we would all crawl from the room. What is written on the screen is who we are, not what we appear to be to man. The inner man is what God grieves over. "For God sees not as man sees, for man looks at the outward appearance, but the Lord looks at the heart" (1 Sam. 16:7).

I was refreshed several years ago by the pastor of a large Pentecostal church who had been caught up in this imaginary world. He said, "I've come full circle. When this new building was erected, I got caught up in all the glitter and glamour. But now the craving of my heart is to have a sovereign move of God. I'm seeking Him, and my congregation is seeking Him, like never before."

The evening service at that church was evidence of his words. What an incredible hunger there was among the people! Hundreds were pursuing the Lord at the altars. Little children sobbed as they watched their moms and dads weep before the Lord. What a wonderful, godly example for them to follow — godly sorrow leading to repentance! How refreshing it was for me to see. And how much more so it must have brought pleasure to the Lord! (By the way, this church was Brownsville Assembly of God, in Pensacola, Florida. On Father's Day, 1995, their prayers were answered. The power of God flooded the church like a mighty river. Hundreds of thousands continue pouring through their doors to receive a touch from the Lord. Tens of thousands have repented and received Jesus Christ as their personal Savior.)

How many respected leaders have fallen headlong to the death of their integrity from the balcony of their conceited castles? They've been poisoned by their positions! What sorrow this must bring to the Lord. He has seen the same pattern for years:

> What fault did your fathers find in me, that they strayed so far from me? They followed worthless idols and became worthless themselves. They did not ask, "Where is the Lord, who brought us up out of Egypt?"...I brought you into a fertile land...But you came and defiled my land and made my inheritance detestable (Jer. 2:5-7, NIV).

Consider the mess we've made of America. Our quest for knowledge has become blatant idolatry. Like Adam and Eve, we want a bite of the fruit of the knowledge of good and evil. We want to become like God. "Knowledge is power," we proclaim in our classrooms.

There is a movement called eugenics, which is devoted to improving the human species by controlling heredity. That's right, we're even experimenting with the cloning of embryos. Now we think the power of life is in our hands! Technology has gone too far. This is not the dawning of the eugenic era; it is the damning of the human era!

Jesus warns it is better to have a heart full of God than a head full of knowledge. "For what is a man profited, if he shall gain the whole world, and lose his own soul?" (Matt. 16:26, KJV). Yet scientists persist in saying that we're on the verge of understanding how creation came into existence. What idolatry! Jeremy Taylor, the seventeenth century Anglican pastor, said, "Can anything in this world be more foolish than to think that all this rare fabric of heaven and earth can come by chance, when all the skill of art is not able to make an oyster?"[14] And Solomon said, "Increasing knowledge results in increasing pain" (Eccl. 1:18). We can pore over archeological books past midnight, but one day we'll face the One who spoke it all into existence. We can idolize our planet, spend billions to save it and lose our own souls. What irony, what idolatry!

> "Why has the Lord done thus to this land and to this house?" And they will say, "Because they forsook the

Lord, the God of their Fathers, who brought them from the land of Egypt, and they adopted other gods, and worshiped them and served them, therefore He has brought all this adversity on them" (2 Chr. 7:21-22).

Recently I confronted a young man about whether he loved Christ. He was seated next to his fiancée, a beautiful girl with whom he was obviously infatuated. The Lord pointed this young man out to me and told me to say, "If you would fall in love with Jesus as much as you love this girl, all heaven would come down in your life." The words gripped his heart, and he began to weep.

Several weeks later, I received a letter from one of his friends. It seems the young man had taken those words as having come directly from the Lord. Jesus was put back on the throne. The young man's prayers once again were being answered. His father, a man who was hardened to the gospel and had rejected it for years, was now back in church and melting in the presence of the Lord.

Anything that takes the place of prominence in our lives is an idol. From lovers to land, from fame to fortune, from golf to game fishing. It's all idolatry when God is shoved to the side. How many men across this continent will rise before dawn to snag a few fish but won't roll out of bed to seek the Lord? How many Christians know more about pursuing a golf ball than pursuing God? How many young people can tell you who won the latest football game but are ashamed to tell their closest friends how not to lose their own souls? Such hypocrisy, such heartbreak!

It's even possible that our desire to be known as holy is a prideful idol. Robert Murray McCheyne once said, "The fame of being a godly man is as great a snare as the fame of being learned or eloquent. It is possible to attend with scrupulous anxiety even to secret habits of devotion, in order to get a name for holiness." He went on to say that most of God's people are contented to be saved from the hell that is without. But they are not so anxious to be saved from the hell that is within.[15]

Cast down your idols; break them into tiny pieces! Let them be crushed to dust under the hammer of the Lord! Please the Lord and soothe His sorrow by becoming a child totally yielded to His Lordship. If you feel the chastising rod of your heavenly Father, thank the Lord! Thank God that He cares. "For whom the Lord loveth he chasteneth" (Heb. 12:6, KJV). John Flavel, an English divine in the

1600s, once said, "Oh how many have been wheeled to hell in the chariots of earthly pleasures, while others have been whipped to heaven by the rod of affliction!"[16]

As we probe the heart of God, as we hear His heartbeat and begin to see life through eternity's eyes, may this teaching grip us and grieve us. Are there other areas of our lives that grieve the Lord? How about a thankless heart? Ingratitude grieves the Lord. I encourage you to get alone with God, pore over the Scriptures and have Him reveal every area that causes Him sorrow. We need to put an end to the unnecessary grief we're causing Him. Please understand that I am writing this book with tears. My desire in writing this chapter and others is to lead us back to the place of contrition and repentance. We have strayed so far and have been mumbling the words of Jeremiah, "I am innocent, surely his anger is turned away from me" (Jer. 2:35). Yet the opposite is true: We have been negligent in our relationship. And "a neglected Savior will be a severe Judge" (Thomas Boston, Scottish Presbyterian minister and writer, 1676–1732).

The flood during the days of Noah was not due to God's grief turned violent. No, we've all read about violent grief. When a grieving father becomes outraged at the light sentence invoked upon the man who raped and killed his daughter, he indulges in irrational, violent grief, killing the rapist. And he finds himself in prison for murder. God's grief is different. It is saturated in love. His behavioral reaction toward His grief is just. He says in Amos 8:9-10: "I will darken the earth in the clear day...I will turn your feasts into mourning, and all your songs into lamentations...and I will make the end thereof as a bitter day" (KJV). We must understand that He has weighed everything in the balance, and His decision is just.

This is the time to weep. We must join the Lord in His brokenness over fallen man. These words from Horatius Bonar cut to readers' hearts over a century ago, and they are still as sharp as if he were walking on the earth today:

> The present seems a time of peculiar warning to the saints.
> Many are lying under the rebukes of the Lord. Judgment
> has begun at the house of God. God is dealing very closely
> and very solemnly with His own. On many a saint, at this
> moment, is His rod lying heavily. For He would fain warn
> and arouse them ere the evil day arrive.

He is dealing with them as He dealt with Lot on the night before the desolation of Sodom. Let the saints, then, be warned. Let them be zealous and repent and do their first works. Come out, be separate, touch not the unclean thing! Put off the works of darkness; put on the armor of light. He is calling them to get up to a higher level in the spiritual life; to have done with wavering, indecision and compromise. He is calling on them to consider the Apostle and High Priest of their profession and walk in His steps. He is calling on them to look at the cloud of witnesses and lay aside every weight, especially that sin which doth so easily beset them and to run with patience the race set before them — "looking unto Jesus."

Church of the living God! Be warned. Please not thyself, even as Jesus pleased not Himself. Live for Him, not for thyself; for Him, not for the world. Walk worthy of thy name and calling; worthy of Him who bought thee as His bride; worthy of thine everlasting inheritance.

Up, too and warn the world! The chastisements that are falling so thickly on thee are forerunners of the fiery shower that is preparing for the earth. Up, then and warn them, urge and entreat them to flee from the gathering wrath. They have no time to lose; neither hast thou. The last storm is on the wing. Its dark skirts are already visible in the heavens. Judgment has begun at the house of God, and if so, then, what shall the end be of them that obey not the gospel of God![17]

God is scanning the earth looking for a few godly men and women. He's searching out the Noahs, the ones who will bring Him pleasure. May the characteristics that were found in Noah be found in us. "But Noah found favor in the eyes of the Lord" (Gen. 6:8).

I trust that right now you are still embracing the Lord. As you do, let's take a look now at why Noah found favor in the eyes of the Lord:

First, he was righteous:

Son of man, when the land sinneth against me by trespassing grievously, then will I stretch out mine hand upon it, and will break the staff of the bread thereof, and will send famine upon it, and will cut off man and beast from it: Though these three men, Noah, Daniel, and Job, were in it, they should deliver but their own souls by their righteousness, saith the Lord God (Ezek. 14:13-14, KJV).

Noah was morally clean. He was a virtuous man, holding forth the standard of the Lord.

Second, Noah was intimate with the Lord. "Noah was a just man and perfect in his generations, and Noah walked with God" (Gen. 6:9, KJV). The original text signifies a continual conversation with the Lord. This is the same word used to describe Enoch's relationship with God. It's interesting that God took Enoch and left Noah!

Third, Noah was obedient. "By faith Noah, being warned by God about things not yet seen, in reverence prepared an ark for the salvation of his household, by which he condemned the world, and became an heir of the righteousness which is according to faith" (Heb. 11:7). Remember, it took Noah more than one hundred years to build the ark. God said to do it; He didn't say how long it would take! Obedience!

"But as the days of Noah were, so shall also the coming of the Son of man be" (Matt. 24:37, KJV). Let's determine to be God's Noah in these final days. Let's turn God's mourning into dancing!

FOUR

BIG BOYS DON'T CRY

*Don't be ashamed to weep —
for your sake and for the sakes
of those around you.*

I call it "pagan programming." Society's sad definition of manhood has produced generation upon generation of "masculine mummies." Grown men, many of whom desperately want to express themselves, are suffocating in the wrappings of an idiotic indoctrination. Sadly this includes most Christian men, the very leaders of the church of Jesus Christ.

Simply put, we have been programmed to "put on." Whatever you do, don't cry! Don't let them see the real you. Quench your emotions! Bite your quivering lip! Change the subject! Turn your head and take slow, deep breaths. Fight the feeling, and it will pass. You'll be marked for life if they see you sob.

My friend, this myth melts under the intense heat of truth. I say to you, let the tears flow, and you will be marked for life. You'll be marked as a man!

What makes a grown man cry? You name it — everything from extreme pleasure to the pits of discouragement. Whether they're grieving the loss of a loved one or simply watching a patriotic parade, men who are in touch with their feelings can be brought to tears.

I want to take a look at some men who cry and why. In his book, *Crying: The Mystery of Tears,* Dr. William H. Frey II states, "It's a rare person who never sheds tears of sorrow, joy, anguish or ecstasy. Throughout the history of humankind, tears have been intertwined with the very essence of the human heart."[1] According to Dr. Frey, the average male cries about once a month. During the course of a good weep, a man secretes a milliliter of tears through as many as sixty eye glands.[2]

Stuart Cosgrove concludes in his article on men who cry:

> The image of men crying cuts to the very core of male identity. According to trite generalization, men rarely cry. In order to preserve the honour of masculinity, they suppress tears and hide their most fragile emotions behind a mask of order and control. Burdened with this myth, when men do break down and cry, it is seen as an event of such profound significance that it begs attention and floods the onlooker with a belief that something important has taken place. But like most images of maleness, holding back the tears is a conceit waiting to be exposed.[3]

Some men want to cry but can't. Physically able, yet bound by years of emotional suppression, they find themselves isolated from their true feelings. "I wish I could cry," confesses G. Modele Clarke:

> I mean really cry. I'm yearning for a wet, noisy, gut-wrenching outpour that comes from deep inside me and releases years of repressed grief and pain. But there is an emotional block — an impenetrable wall — that stands between me and my tears. Whenever I discuss my inability to cry, I make the distinction between ability and desire. Believe me, I would if I could.[4]

Some men who claim to be unable to cry have found themselves suddenly teary-eyed in a dark movie theater during an emotional, heartwrenching scene. Yet even in the darkness, they quickly brush away any evidence of their apparent "weakness."

One of America's contemporary heroes, General Norman Schwarzkopf, openly displays emotions. He says, "I don't think I would like a man who is incapable of enough emotion to get tears in his eyes. That type of person scares me. That's not a human being."[5]

An entire book could be written on weeping warriors. Many heroes of our country, brave in battle and powerful in public, have displayed their feelings without remorse. Many a soldier on bended knee has kissed the ground and dripped tears of joy as his term of foreign duty concluded. And the bystanders who shared in his victory wept as well. Their emotions welled up indescribably as the Marine band played, "God bless America, land that I love."

History records innumerable moments of unforgettable emotion. Millions of eyes were moistened by tears at the conclusion of one of the most noted prayers in our nation's existence. It took place at the advent of what was to be the conclusion of World War II, D-Day. The entire nation had their radios tuned in as President Franklin D. Roosevelt prayed: "Almighty God: Our sons, pride of our nation, this day have set upon a mighty endeavor, a struggle to preserve our republic, our religion and our civilization, and to set free a suffering humanity. Lead them straight and true; give strength to their arms, stoutness to their hearts, steadfastness in their faith."[6]

Men and women listened to the prayer as they sat in their own homes, homes from which their loved ones had gone forth to fight for freedom. Then came the closing words, followed by two song selections that gripped even the strongest of men, melting them to tears: "Thy will be done, almighty God. Amen." The pause was brief. Then, from the radio came a chorus of voices reverently singing:

Onward, Christian soldiers,
Marching as to war,
With the cross of Jesus
Going on before![7]

At the conclusion of this emotional hymn, the beloved singer Julia Ward Howe came on. Across the airwaves she sang the hymn that struck the heart of every American:

Mine eyes have seen the glory
    of the coming of the Lord,
He is trampling out the vintage
    where the grapes of wrath are stored;

He hath loosed the fateful lightning
 of His terrible swift sword —
His truth is marching on.

All across America, an emotional choir of voices in millions of living rooms joined in at the chorus: "Glory, glory, hallelujah! Glory, glory, hallelujah! Glory, glory, hallelujah! His truth is marching on!" Each of the verses was sung. A male voice rendered one verse, a woman's voice the next. Then they united with the entire chorus in the closing verse. How unforgettably impressive!

In the beauty of the lilies
Christ was born across the sea,
With a glory in His bosom
 that transfigures you and me;
As He died to make men holy,
 let us live to make men free
While God is marching on.[8]

Across the country, grown men squalled like babies. Entire families wept uncontrollably. This incredible, patriotic moment in America's history moved men to tears.

Men also have been brought to tears by overwhelming grief. Only a few days before his untimely death, President Abraham Lincoln told of the way in which the peace of heaven flooded his heart. It happened through the death of his son.

As his boy lay dying, Lincoln saw his usually strong reason come to the brink of peril. He stayed up night after night — elbows on his knees, face in his hands — praying, "Father, if it be possible, let this cup pass from me."

A nurse, Miss Ida Tarbell, was with the president when the dreaded blow fell. They stood with their heads bowed low, staring into death. Grief gripped Lincoln's heart.

"This was the most severe trial of my life. I was not a Christian," he explained. Miss Tarbell, herself having experienced deep human sorrow and divine comfort, pointed the weeping president to her Savior. His private sorrow at that moment prepared him for the tremendous public sorrow about to come.

"When I went to Gettysburg," Lincoln said, "and saw the graves of thousands of our soldiers, I then and there consecrated myself to

Christ." With teary eyes he told his friends that at last he had found the faith he'd longed for. He realized, he said, that his heart was changed and that he loved the Savior.[9] Imagine it! The president of the United States weeping at the cross.

Hulking President Lyndon Johnson cried intensely when he stood beside Gandhi's grave in India. In 1978, the year in which he finally lost his battle with cancer, Hubert Humphrey wept in public several times. At one point he made this often-quoted remark: "A man without tears is a man without a heart."[10]

When the great zeppelin Hindenburg came crashing to the ground in New Jersey in the 1930s, the nation was horrified by the sounds of the commentator's sobs as he watched burning bodies attempting to escape the wreckage.

From national sports figures to politicians, from war heroes to business executives, our nation witnesses a continual trail of visible tears. Great men throughout the centuries have shed the fear of man and bathed themselves in tears.

Dr. Frey's research lists a virtual catalog of tearful men. The baseball star Babe Ruth cried in front of sixty thousand fans at Yankee Stadium when he was recovering from cancer. The actor James Stewart cried on American television when his dog died. Richard Nixon cried over Watergate. Leonard Bernstein cried with artistic emotion when he conducted at the Kennedy Center in Washington. President Bill Clinton was seen nationwide wiping tears from his eyes on Inauguration Day as he enjoyed an inspirational gospel song.

Only God knows how many men were shocked out of their emotional slumber on November 22, 1963. The shots were heard around the world: President John F. Kennedy was dead. It was a day of public openness — grown men could weep without remorse.

The American evangelist Charles Finney wrote of his own struggle with tears:

> I took down my bass-violin, and as I was accustomed to do, began to play and sing some pieces of sacred music. But as soon as I began to sing those sacred works, I began to weep. It seemed as if my heart was all liquid; and my feelings were in such a state that I could not hear my own voice in singing without causing my sensibility to over flow. I wondered at this and tried to suppress my tears, but

could not. After trying in vain to suppress my tears, I put up my instrument and stopped singing.[11]

Finney had written earlier in his journal of his inability to shed tears. Another great man, another weeper.

The list is endless; the facts are clear: Big boys do cry. This brings us to the most significant example of all.

Jesus Himself wept (see John 11:35; Luke 19:41). Few would dispute His manhood. He had worked by the sweat of His brow as His carpenter-father had taught Him. He could swing an ax like a lumberjack. The sweet music of His carpenter's saw could be heard from sunup to sundown. Heavy stones and cumbersome beams yielded to His determination. He was a blue-collar worker.

Over the years, His hands grew rough. Calluses formed over boyish skin, muscles bulged as He toiled into years of manhood. Outwardly, He was a man's man, yet inwardly, He had a tenderness that soon would shock the world. He had felt every pain any man would ever feel. He was tempted in every way. And He was tested and found spotless.

His following would be the envy of any politician. He became the table talk of the wealthy. But the supposedly righteous became outraged because He surrounded Himself with the common man. The multitudes hung on His every word. "No man speaks like this man," they proclaimed. "It's as if He knows us." His words were as sweet as honey to some, as bitter as gall to others. Like you and me, He had both friends and enemies.

They saw Him heal the sick and raise the dead. The lame jumped up in joy and victory. The lifelong blind saw the light of day. Mercy was shown to the downtrodden. The people liked that, but they were just as startled when He declared harsh judgment upon the self-righteous.

You can almost hear the people thinking: *This man is incredible. He doesn't care what people appear to be. He shoots for the heart! It's as if He knows His destiny and ours. He stands up when most of us would cower off.* Yes, Jesus was a hero. The bravest man alive — ever. Yet He was not afraid to cry.

The secret? Simple. Consider these things:

He spoke the truth in love under the anointing of God. He learned obedience and yielded to the Father's plan for His life. He saw everything through the eyes of eternity. He understood that bitterness toward His enemies or pride about His successes would destroy every-thing His Father had sent Him to build.

In order to carry out His divine mandate, Jesus knew the necessity of remaining in touch with His feelings. He knew when to get angry and when to show compassion. He knew when to express joy and when to weep. He understood the language of tears. His emotional life was under control, yet it was in plain sight for all to see.

Jesus shattered the modern myth of manhood. Yes, strong men have feelings, and they show them. Jesus, David, Jeremiah, Paul, Timothy and John were all great men and heroes of the faith and all weepers. From these examples, we see that true men are honest with their gut emotions. Big boys do cry!

In his timely book, *Prepare for Revival,* Rob Warner emphasizes the weepers in the Word:

> The Bible is one place where it's certainly not the case that big boys never cry. As to individuals who weep, we find a biblical who's who. Esau wept in his rivalry with Jacob (Gen. 27:38). Jacob wept with Esau in a wary reconciliation (Gen. 33:4), and later wept at the presumed death of his son Joseph (Gen. 37:35). When Joseph was preparing to reveal his true identity to his brothers, he wept so loudly that it became a talking point among the Egyptians (Gen. 45:2). Soon he wept with his brothers (Gen. 45:14-15), and when Jacob finally arrived in Egypt, Joseph threw his arms around his father and "wept for a long time" (Gen. 46:29). Later, he wept over Jacob's corpse and wept again over his father's last request to forgive his brothers fully (Gen. 50:1,17). Saul, the first king of Israel, wept (1 Sam. 24:16), as did David and Jonathan (1 Sam. 20:41). On one occasion David's army wept aloud all day long until they had no strength left within them (1 Sam. 30:4). Above all, Jeremiah is the prophet of tears. He frequently weeps for Israel, even as he brings dire warnings of impending judgment, and cries out for mercy in tears (Jer. 9:1,18; 14:17; Lam. 1:16; 3:48). Peter wept bitterly after his threefold denial of Christ (Matt. 26:75). Paul also knew the place and value of tears. He described his ministry as serving the Lord with great humility and tears (Acts 20:19), and he

continually warned with tears against false teachers (Acts 20:31). When Paul wrote to Timothy he remembered with fondness Timothy's tears at their last meeting (2 Tim. 1:4).[12]

Yes, when true men are honest with their gut emotions, the tears flow freely. Throughout this book, you'll probe even deeper into the lives of weepers in the Word.

From their early childhood most boys are taught to disguise their deep emotions. This teaching is not new. For centuries men have been held captive by their inhibitions. Hiding or suppressing tears has been a common reaction among them for ages. Those men who "couldn't control themselves" often have been deemed weaklings and compared with crying babies or teary-eyed women.

Countless proverbs and deep-rooted cultural beliefs have helped to fuel these attitudes. An old adage from India gives this warning: "A laughing woman and a crying man should never be trusted." How typical of this deeply inbred indoctrination. "Stop crying and act like a man!" has been the counsel to millions of young boys across this land. Many fathers (and some mothers) feared their sons would grow up to be sissies and wrongly associated their tears with weakness.

A friend of mine working in Thailand recently told me that in the Thai culture tears are indeed a sign of weakness. Seeing Thai men with tears in their eyes is a rarity.

In Italy, crying in public is more socially acceptable than in the United States. In Japan and Britain crying is considered taboo for all people, but especially for men.

Jeri and I lived in Granada, Spain, for six months. The most popular tourist attraction in our area was the Alhambra. This incredible, Moorish fortress stands majestically over the city. It speaks of power. Its outside was built to withstand the most intense warfare. The inside, with its intricate mosaics, stately rooms and spectacular gardens, has drawn admirers from around the world.

Just outside the city stands a hotel called the Sigh of the Moor. There is a very telling story behind it. In 1492, King Ferdinand and the Christian armies of Spain ousted Moorish King Boabdil and expelled him from Southern Spain. From high atop this hill, the majestic Alhambra can be clearly seen. History records that on this spot, while leaving Granada, King Boabdil's mother publicly humiliated her son by openly stating, "You cry like a woman because you do not know how to defend yourself like a man."[13] It was a perfect example of public response when the "mask of manhood" slips off.

Fear of this type of public humiliation has been the culprit behind many a man's quenching of his true emotions. To my surprise, on many occasions men have come up to me after I've led a tear-soaked evangelistic meeting and said, "Doesn't it bother you to be so open with people? Your tears seem to flow so freely. I could never be so transparent."

Roberta Israeloff concluded from her research on tears:

> The world is pretty much divided into two camps. In one are those people for whom weeping is as natural a response as scratching an itch, who believe in the medicinal value of a good cry and aren't unhinged when others indulge in tears. Then there are those who hate to cry and who turn away from the tears of others. Weepers make them suspicious.[14]

Camp number two is crowded with men. Rarely a week goes by for them without a visit to this camp. A typical example would be my recent encounter with a young twenty-year-old named David.

Early one morning I found myself banging on this notorious gang member's front door, led by a compassion to see him come to Jesus. Everyone had told me of his evil exploits and impossible nature. A good friend had explained to me that David had a good heart, but it had been buried in rebellion, drugs, fighting and parties. My goal that day was to bypass all superficiality and reach the soil of his heart.

My conversation with David was quick and to the point. He had received a copy of my testimony entitled *Stone Cold Heart* and, already aware of my background, he listened to me openly. Outwardly he appeared hard, but his eyes told another story. Upon explaining the hypocrisy of wearing a mask, I noticed a marked change in his countenance. David knew that trying to cover his emotions was futile.

He began to weep. Inwardly, I rejoiced at the realization that David was not as hard as everyone perceived. The strong man lurking deep within his heart was giving way to the power of truth. The walls were weakening. Resisting now was out of the question. After a prayer with us, David pleaded, "Don't give up on me. I'm coming around."

In the 1700s Thomas Scott wrote about the strong man who dwells within. Upon reading these lines, you will discover, as I did, an incredible fortress — an Alhambra — that surrounds the stately rooms of our heart:

> A certain person once said of me, that I was like a stone rolling down a hill, which could neither be stopped nor turned. This witness was true. The strong man armed with my natural pride and obstinacy, with my vain imaginations and reasonings and high thoughts, had built himself many strongholds and kept his castle in my heart. When one stronger than he came against him he stood a long siege: till, being by superior force driven from one to another, and all his armor in which he trusted being at length taken from him, he was constrained to recede. So the Lord having made me willing in the day of his power, I was forced to confess, "O Lord, thou art stronger than I, and hast prevailed" (Jer. 20:7).[15]

The truth that Thomas Scott was referring to, of course, was the truth of Scripture. He had come to the conclusion that nothing precedes it, adds to it or follows it. The Word of God stands alone and remains for eternity. Heaven and earth will pass away, but the Word of the Lord will abide forever.

Right now, I ask every man who is reading this book to reprogram himself, using the Word of God as his guide. Escape this evil education. Be honest — flee the fake. Grasp hold of God!

Dr. Frey encourages men to begin the road back by trying to reclaim their emotions and connect with their deep feelings, as he did: "I stopped crying at about twelve years of age and do not remember crying at all during the next twelve years. I do not know why I stopped and do not recall making a conscious effort to stop — I just stopped."[16] Now at a place where he can once again weep, he counsels others to give themselves permission to feel sadness and pain and to let the tears flow.

I want to add this advice: Consider the value of joining in the sorrow of others. Earnestly try to feel their pain. Hurt with them. Share in a conversation of tears.

Richard Foster, in his book on prayer, encourages those who can't seem to weep outwardly to shed tears before God at least in their intention. Have a weeping heart. Keep your soul in tears. Even if your eyes are dry, your mind and spirit can be broken before God.[17]

Don't be ashamed to weep. For your sake — and the sakes of those around you — shake off society's wrappings. Allow the Lord to break through the logjam of lies. Let the river of tears flow freely.

God can transform you from a masculine mummy to a purposeful man. Let all that is macho melt in the presence of the Lord. Get in touch with your true feelings. Quench not the deep workings of His Spirit. The myth of manhood will melt under the intense heat of truth. Let the tears flow and you will be marked for life. You'll be marked as a man.

Let's pray:

> Dear Jesus, I'm exhausted. I'm so tired of playing this game. I want to open myself to experience everything You have to offer. If tears well up inside, I want them to flow outwardly. Forgive me for holding back years of emotion. You, dear Lord, are the greatest man who ever lived, and I want to follow Your example. You often were moved to tears. I want to experience that same release.
>
> I give to You my heart and life. Heal the hurts. Melt the walls around my heart. I want to experience every part of the abundant life You came to offer. In the precious name of Jesus, Amen.

FIVE

DRY-EYE SYNDROME

Is it possible to be physically incapable of shedding tears?

J eff was eighteen years of age. With tears in his eyes, he explained how for more than a decade he had been unable to weep. Now rejoicing at his newfound freedom, Jeff exclaimed, "This is the first time in years I've been able to openly display my innermost feelings." He told me, "Thank you for coming. Thank you for letting me know it's okay to cry."

Jeff's words echoed the poignant feelings of millions. The majority of us would love to be unshackled from our inhibitions. Embarrassment has become our enemy; we want to be delivered from our self-righteous dignity. Multitudes want to be set free.

At the conclusion of a church service in Atlanta, Georgia, I encountered a man who confessed to me, "There is something inside of me that wants to come out. It's as if I were about to burst. I'm supposed to cry, but I just can't. Please pray for me; I want to weep."

Perhaps this book can serve as a personal emancipation proclamation for those caught in the slavery of tearlessness. Many of us have a heart that weeps silently in the desire to have freedom of expression. And I believe those chains need to snap. I pray that, in reading this book, you will walk out the prison doors and enter the free world.

Still many people wonder, *Is it possible to be physically incapable of shedding tears? If so, can it be cured?* Another common question is, What causes tears? And do we benefit physically from crying?

Medical science has made incredible strides in the study of tears. In the next few pages, I'll try to present answers to these inquiries. The information I provide here is drawn from years of research by the most respected physicians in this field. In particular, Dr. William Frey's book, *Crying: The Mystery of Tears,* has been an invaluable resource in my research on weeping.[1] I highly recommend it for those desiring a deeper understanding of what's behind our tears. Yet, even so, researchers admit we're only beginning to comprehend the mystery of tears.

The title of this chapter, "Dry-Eye Syndrome," speaks of an actual medical condition in which our eyes are unable to produce tears. Yet this condition is not as common as many non-weepers would like to believe. Many of us are quick to categorize our insecurities, often passing the buck to a physical infirmity when the actual cure is at our fingertips.

Indeed, research has proved that many who claim to have dry eyes can be detected in a dark theater during an emotional, tear-jerking scene wiping tears from their eyes. Their hearts are gripped; their emotions enthralled; and under the covering of darkness, their inhibitions fade. If this describes you, then your problem could be one of pride more than anything else.

Let's take a look at some of the basic questions people have concerning crying and tears.

WHAT ARE TEARS?

According to the American Medical Association, tears are the salty, watery secretion produced by the lacrimal glands, part of the lacrimal apparatus of the eye. The tear film over the cornea and the conjunctiva consists of three layers: an inner, mucous layer secreted by glands in the conjunctiva; an intermediate layer of salt water; and an outer, oily layer secreted by the meibomian glands.[2]

A deficiency in tear production causes keratoconjunctivitis sicca (dry-eye syndrome). Excessive tear production may cause watering eye.

Tears help wash the eye of potentially harmful germs. I can't help noticing the spiritual parallel here: Tears, in our crying out to God, can wash our spiritual eyes of any evil that has taken root. Just as the physical tears wash the dangerous germs, so our spiritual tears serve as cleansing, falling to the ground and taking the harmful germs with them.

Is There Such a Thing as Artificial Tears?

Yes. Artificial tears are preparations used to supplement inadequate production of tears in keratoconjunctivitis sicca and other conditions causing dryness of the eyes. To be effective, artificial tears must be applied at frequent intervals. Artificial tears may also be used to relieve discomfort caused by irritants, such as smoke or dust, but they provide only temporary relief.

Many preparations contain a preservative that can irritate the eyes. Contaminated preparations may cause serious eye infections.[3]

Why Do Babies Cry?

Crying is the only way a baby has to communicate. At that age, crying is the only way your small baby has to get your attention. The most common causes for babies crying are hunger, gas, general discomfort, pain, teething, boredom and loneliness.

"If parents only understood," says S. Norman Sherry, M.D., "that crying is a normal part of a baby's development — that if a baby doesn't cry, then something is really wrong — maybe they wouldn't worry so much."[4]

Interestingly, infant crying has come under scrutiny lately because of its clinical importance in understanding maternal distress. That is, many women become so distraught by their babies' crying — and their own inability to comfort them — that their self-esteem and confidence in their mothering skills plummet. They may stop breast-feeding or in extreme cases be pushed to abuse their children.

WHAT OCCURS WHEN WE CRY?

When you experience intense emotions, such as grief or anger, your brain sends a signal to your lacrimal glands. These glands are located over each eye and behind each eyelid. Tears, in the form of a watery, salty fluid, are produced continuously from these glands. Each time you blink, your eyelids draw fluid from the lacrimal glands. Continuous tears constantly bathe your cornea, the curved, clear front of your eye.

This flow, medically known as lacrimation, serves to keep the eye clean and germ-free and to lubricate the movement of the eyelid over the eyeball. Every time the eyelid blinks, the fluid drains away into small holes in the inner corner of the eye, down the tear duct, to the back of the nose and throat. But when you laugh or cry, or if the eye is irritated by a foreign body such as dust or grit, lacrimation increases and there is an overflow of tears.[5]

IS THERE MORE THAN ONE KIND OF TEAR?

Yes, there are two kinds of tears. Every time we blink, a film bathes the surface of the eye with a bacteria-fighting fluid. Anyone who has chopped onions is familiar with irritant tears, which dilute and flush away the strong onion vapors. When a foreign object such as a loose eyelash or grain of sand gets in our eyes, these tears help to wash away the irritating invaders. This is called neurogenic lacrimation.

The second type of tear is uniquely human. These are emotional tears, and they fall under the category of psychic lacrimation. Although weeping is usually associated with sorrow, human tears appear in response to many types of emotional stress. From tears of grief when a loved one dies, to extreme joy from winning a game, tears play an important part in human emotions.

Emotional crying starts in the part of your brain that governs emotions, memory and behavior. If a surgeon blocks the nerves in this area, you won't be able to produce emotional tears, yet it would have no effect on the other kinds of tears your body produces.

Continuous and irritant tears are controlled by different nerves than those that affect emotional tearing. If those nerves are cut, or if a doctor places an anesthetic on the surface of your eye, continuous and irritant tears stop. But there would be no such change in emotional tears.

Is There Such a Thing as Cryophobia?

Yes, but it does not refer to the fear of crying. Cryophobia is actually the fear of extremely cold temperatures, cold objects or ice. However, in *The Encyclopedia of Phobias, Fears and Anxieties,* which lists over two thousand known phobias and fears, we do find the fear of crying. Some individuals who are quick to cry in uncomfortable situations may avoid such situations because they fear others will see them cry. They may fear criticism for their tearful reactions.[6]

Why Does It Seem That Girls Cry More Than Boys?

Before they hit puberty, girls and boys cry about the same amount. But by age eighteen, women cry more often, says Dr. Frey. Biology may be partly responsible for this gender gap. Dr. Frey points out that after puberty, women's blood levels of prolactin (which is found in tears) are 60 percent higher than men's. After menopause, a woman's prolactin level drops. This could explain why postmenopausal women are most likely to have dry-eye syndrome.[7]

Many experts still believe that cultural conditioning is a major cause. "Boys learn early on to deaden their awareness to two types of emotions," says psychologist Ronald Levant, Ed. D., clinical supervisor of Couples and Family Center at Harvard Medical School's Cambridge Hospital. "They shut off both vulnerable feelings — such as hurt, disappointment, sadness and fear — and tender ones, such as compassion, warmth and affection." Which leaves what? "Anger and lust."

"As a result, when painful emotions arise, many men explode in rage," explains Dr. Levant. "Others run from these feelings or squelch them."[8]

How Can I Stop Myself From Crying?

When you do need to keep tears in check, the best way is to take slow, deep breaths, fighting the hyperventilation that accompanies and exacerbates crying. Also, you can try shifting your gaze. Tipping your head back restrains tears. Or simply looking away from whatever is making you cry can help you keep calm.

"Crying is a natural reaction when you're sad, joyful or even surprised. But if you find yourself crying repeatedly about the same problems," says Dr. Frey, "you may need to address the underlying cause. Shedding tears isn't a permanent solution."[9]

In my research on tears I came across an article about a female firefighter in Portsmouth, Virginia.

"Cry, even once...never!" says Jeanette Hentze, a mother of two who has been a firefighter for almost three years. Hentze had been trained in Critical Incident Stress Debriefing, a technique to help firefighters and other emergency workers deal with the pressures of their jobs. "It was really hard keeping up the male standard," she confessed. "But I was determined — I had to show them I could do the job without breaking down."[10]

But now that she's proven herself, Hentze feels it's OK — even necessary — to show her emotions. Recently, she cried after returning from an emergency medical run during which she and her partner worked futilely to resuscitate a woman who had collapsed while at home with her twelve-year-old son. "I'd never dealt with a child watching his mother die. That hit home. And by crying, I was able to let it out. I felt a load had been lifted." She added that she thought if more of her male coworkers could cry, they wouldn't have the long-term effects of bottling up their feelings. More and more women and men would agree, "Enough with this business that tears are for wimps, something to be ashamed of. It's time crying got the respect it deserves."[11]

IS IT PHYSICALLY DANGEROUS TO HOLD BACK TEARS OF EMOTION?

Chronically holding back tears can build stress, increasing your risk of tension-related problems, such as insomnia and acne. Stress causes a change in our body's chemistry. People generally feel better after crying. Perhaps the reason for the relief we feel after a good cry is that weeping removes chemicals that were built up as a result of emotional stress.

Suppose a person inhibits sobbing by deliberate contraction of his diaphragm, and this becomes habitual and unnoticed. If this happens, the organism will lose both activities — that is, the man who manipulates his functioning in this way can neither sob nor breathe freely. Unable to sob, he never releases and finishes with his sadness. Crying is a genuine need of a human organism which has sustained loss, and the sadness will often be released by crying it out once and for all.[12]

Dr. Erick Linderman, psychiatrist-in-chief of the Massachusetts General Hospital and a pioneer in the investigation of repressed sorrow, tells of a young nurse who tended her father through the long winter of his final illness. She was very devoted to her father, and often she fought back tears as she nursed him.

When he died, a well-meaning friend sternly forbade her to show any grief for the sake of her mother, who had a weak heart. Within hours, the emotionally repressed nurse developed a case of ulcerated colitis. She slowly corroded inwardly because of her nervous system. Eventually she died — killed by the suppressed grief she would not allow herself to express in copious tears.[13]

WHAT IS DRY-EYE SYNDROME, AND HOW CAN A PERSON KNOW IF HE HAS IT?

Known in the medical field as keratoconjunctivitis sicca, dry-eye syndrome is a condition marked by hyperemia of the conjunctiva, lacrimal deficiency, thickening of the corneal epithelium, itching and burning of the eye and often reduced visual acuity.[14]

This disorder is more common among the elderly. A wide range of conditions is characterized by dry eyes. Hypofunction of the lacrimal glands, causing loss of the aqueous component of tears, may be due to aging, hereditary disorders, systemic disease or systemic and topical drugs. Excessive evaporation of tears may be due to environmental factors such as hot, dry and/or windy climate. It can also be caused by abnormalities of the lipid component of the tear film. Mucin deficiency may be due to malnutrition, infection, burns or drugs.

Treatment depends on the cause. In most early cases, the corneal and conjunctival epithelial changes are reversible. Aqueous deficiency can be treated by replacement of the aqueous component of tears with various types of artificial tears. Mucin deficiency can be partially compensated for by the use of the patient's own serum as local eye drops.[15]

It is possible through an injury to lose your capacity for tears. An example is nineteen-year-old Iris Clark of London. She was unable to weep with joy after she had won $33,900 in a court suit. She had been struck down by a truck three years before, and through the resulting head injury, she can no longer weep.[16]

Dr. William Frey warns against holding back tears of frustration, anger or pain. Those emotional tears may be carrying away far more than grief. Tears can help relieve stress by ridding the body of potentially harmful chemicals that are produced in times of stress.[17]

To support this theory, Dr. Frey and his colleagues compared emotionally induced tears to tears that were produced in response to eye irritation, such as those caused by peeling onions.

"So far, we know that the two types of tears have different chemical compositions," Dr. Frey reported. "But we haven't as yet identified the specific chemicals related to emotional stress. We do know, however, that people feel better after crying. In one survey, 85 percent of women and 73 percent of men reported that they generally felt better. On the other hand, those who hold back tears may be at greater risk for stress-related disorders, such as ulcers and colitis."[18]

In a recent experiment done at the Marquette University College of Nursing in Milwaukee, Wisconsin, researchers studied one hundred men and women with those stress-related disorders. They were then compared to fifty healthy volunteers.

The doctors found that those with ulcers and colitis were more likely to regard crying as a sign of weakness or loss of control than the healthy group of people.[19]

Dr. Frey concludes by saying, "It seems to me that people should cry if they want to. Emotional tears are a uniquely human occurrence, and I doubt that they can be passed off as incidental or purposeless."[20]

In closing this chapter, I'd like to tell you about a counseling session held some three hundred years ago. The counselor was a godly man; the counselee, a distraught non-weeper who desired to cry. The condition had not yet been labeled keratoconjunctivitis sicca, or dry-eye syndrome, but the patient had all the symptoms. The understanding pastor didn't have at his disposal the latest medical studies on eye diseases; instead, he reached into his heart for the answer.

Reverend Thomas Fuller was considered one of the wisest divines of the seventeenth century. It is said of his preaching and ministry that people flocked to hear him as bees to honey, sitting even in doorways and windows to listen to his encouraging gospel message. They devoured his messages and craved his counsel.

One particular young man was concerned over his inability to weep. He said to Reverend Fuller, "I have by nature such dry eyes that they will afford no moisture to bemoan my sins."

Believing the man to be sincere, Reverend Fuller responded:

> Then it is a natural defect, and no moral default, so by consequence a suffering, and no sin which God will punish. God doth not expect the pipe should run water where He put none into the cistern. Know also, their hearts may be fountains whose eyes are flints, and may inwardly bleed, who do not outwardly weep. Besides, Christ was sent to preach comfort, not to such only as weep, but mourn in Zion. Yea, if thou canst squeeze out no liquid, offer to God the empty bottles, instead of tears, tender and present thine eyes unto Him. And though thou art water-bound, be not wind-bound also; sigh where thou canst not sob, and let thy lungs do what thine eyes cannot perform.[21]

Six

Something to Cry About

We must answer God's call to tears —
with one ear hearing the sweet music
of heaven and with the other,
the moans of hell

I have been accused at times of blatantly presenting the truth. My unabashed proclamation of God's Word comes from having seen both sides very clearly. I admit we are all in the school of God, and no one has more to learn than I do. However, while I don't claim to have all the answers, I have seen enough to make a sound judgment.

The kingdom of darkness was my terrain for many years. Most of my friends danced with the devil and gave their lives to the father of lies. They laughed at his jokes — until they found out the joke was on them. Many are in prison today; others fell headlong into Lucifer's fiery grave.

I suppose I'm guilty of swinging the pendulum far to one side to graphically illustrate the truth of Christ. In many open-air meetings, I've seen sinners cry out as the following announcement was made: "You've heard the gospel. There is nothing more to say. I've done my duty to God and to you. As of this moment, I am no longer responsible for your soul. With tears in my eyes, I am washing your blood from my hands."

I rest my statement, of course, on the truth found in the book of Ezekiel:

> Son of man, I have appointed you a watchman to the house of Israel; whenever you hear a word from My mouth, warn them from Me. When I say to the wicked, "You shall surely die"; and you do not warn him or speak out to warn the wicked from his wicked way that he may live, that wicked man shall die in his iniquity, but his blood I will require at your hand. Yet if you have warned the wicked, and he does not turn from his wickedness or from his wicked way, he shall die in his iniquity; but you have delivered yourself (Ezek. 3:17-19).

This may appear harsh to some, but to others it's just the hard facts. As for me, I'd rather hear the hard truth and live than to fall for a soft lie and die.

From Genesis to Revelation we find blessings and cursings, mercy and judgment, evil and good, and yes, even prosperity and poverty. The Bible speaks of love for the sinner while it boldly condemns his sinfulness. God's Word speaks of heaven without giving any less attention to its counterpart, hell. We hear Jesus speak of the joys of eternity above, while in the same breath He warns of weeping and gnashing of teeth below.

Balance is one key to the Christian life; we need to learn to eat our brussel sprouts along with our Twinkies. What may seem "a hard word" to a Christian is often a "word from God" to an unbeliever. Serious sinners can swallow truth much better than many seasoned saints can. I've received my share of hugs from teary-eyed young people who have said, "Thanks for not leaving me alone. I needed to hear what you had to say. It hurt, but it was the truth." I've been embraced by the backslidden elderly as they whispered in my ear, "Keep preaching the truth, son."

Ultimately, we all must face facts. And perhaps by swinging the pendulum far to one side, we can strike a balance in our views of the church and the world.

Can you remember your father saying, "Stop your whining, or I'll give you something to cry about"? This was, in most cases, just an empty threat, a vain attempt to stop our constant whimpering over some selfish little problem.

Now, imagine for a moment our heavenly Father looking down at our selfish behavior. He frowns at our continual whimpering and whining. Our baby cries have taken their toll on His ears. So He sternly bellows out His judgment: "Stop your whimpering. Let me give you something to cry about."

This Father reaches down and gently lifts our heads. Our misty eyes focus on a filthy child, covered with flies, eating dinner in a waste dump. Then He focuses our attention on blood-stained snow where little children were massacred, victims fallen to man's desire for power. From there we journey with the omnipresent One to a garbage can filled with fetuses. "Take a look at what I see everyday," He says. "Soak up the savagery. Stare at the suffering until your eyes are blood red. Mourn for a minute."

Without another word, our Father concludes by flashing before us thousands of Christian martyrs — some burned alive, others fed to starving beasts, all for the love of Christ. We are reminded that one day we will sit across the table from these triumphant saints. Will we have anything to talk about? Could we even make conversation with them? What if the subject of suffering comes up? We begin to see the point, and our whining suddenly ceases. Our Father has given us something very serious to cry about.

Many today are in a constant state of mourning — not over the suffering or death of some loved one, but over the near death of our old man — self. We live between two worlds. Our sorrow over what we might be giving up in this life is a sure sign of not having fully entered into the other. Yes, we want Jesus, but we cleave to the old man. Our commitment to Christ is seasoned with covenant clauses: "I'll serve You if I can have this..." "I'll follow You if You let me do this..."

We weep more from the brokenness of our bank account than from any brokenness of heart. The prophet Hosea said it well: "They do not cry to Me from their heart when they wail on their beds; for the sake of grain and new wine they assemble themselves, they turn away from Me" (Hos. 7:14).

The rising tide of evil speaks to all of us that something is desperately wrong. We are not advancing, nor are we holding back the flood. We seem merely to have a finger in the dike while other leaks are popping out all over. We are at best only maintaining.

I wonder, *Where is the church triumphant in this desperate time? Where is the church that storms the gates of hell?* We weep, whimper and whine as we dine with God while sinners are choking at the table of devils! We loathe the manna God gives while the world scrapes the barrel for just one grain of wheat. We're no different from the children of Israel:

> The sons of Israel wept again and said, "Who will give us meat to eat? We remember the fish which we used to eat free in Egypt, the cucumbers and the melons and the leeks and the onions and the garlic, but now our appetite is gone. There is nothing at all to look at except this manna."...Now Moses heard the people weeping throughout their families [not over their spiritual condition but rather their own bellies], each man at the doorway of his tent; and the anger of the Lord was kindled greatly, and Moses was displeased (Num. 11:4-6,10).

We haven't learned from Israel's mistakes. Listen once again to the Word of the Lord:

> For I do not want you to be unaware, brethren, that our fathers were all under the cloud, and all passed through the sea; and all were baptized into Moses in the cloud and in the sea; and all ate the same spiritual food; and all drank the same spiritual drink, for they were drinking from a spiritual rock which followed them; and the rock was Christ.
>
> Nevertheless, with most of them God was not well-pleased; for they were laid low in the wilderness. Now these things happened as examples for us, that we should not crave evil things, as they also craved. And do not be idolaters, as some of them were; as it is written, "The people sat down to eat and drink, and stood up to play" (1 Cor. 10:1-7).

Could we stop our sniffling for a few minutes? Our heavenly Father would have us see suffering through His eyes.

I'd like to share with you a story from the *Associated Press*. My initial reaction upon reading this article was one of disbelief; my second emotion was one of overwhelming sadness. The story is fact, not fable.

The young woman's tale was unbelievably gruesome and bizarre — so much so, in fact, that she says police twice brushed her off...The family's darkest secrets remained hidden until last month [Oct. 1993], when detectives got a call from Theresa, now twenty-two and living in Utah.

Suesan was the first to die. During an argument, perhaps as early as 1982, Cross grabbed a handgun and shot Suesan [her daughter] in the chest, Theresa said. The bullet lodged in her back, but she recovered without medical help.

In 1984, at age seventeen, Suesan said she wanted to leave home. Cross [her mother] agreed under one condition: Suesan must let her remove the bullet from her back, Theresa said. That way, if she ever were to report abuse, there would be no corroborating evidence.

The kitchen floor was the operating table; whiskey the anesthetic. Cross dug the bullet out of her daughter's back with a scalpel, Theresa said.

An infection set in, and Suesan grew delirious. Cross decided they had to get rid of her, so she enlisted the aid of William and Robert [her two sons] to dispose of their sister, Theresa said.

They drove Suesan one hundred miles into the Sierra Nevada, turning off the highway near the Squaw Valley ski area. There, they laid her down, doused her with gasoline and burned her alive, Theresa said.

Sheila was next. During an argument with her mother in 1985, Sheila was beaten, handcuffed and forced into a narrow closet, Theresa said.

Theresa, thirteen at the time, recalls hearing her twenty-year-old half-sister moaning and crying, "Help me, help me." But nobody opened the door, she said.

After a few days, the cries stopped, and after a week or so, the stench of rotting flesh filled the apartment.

Cross enlisted her sons for another trip to the mountains, where they left Sheila's body lying by the road in a cardboard box, Theresa said.

The odor of death hung in the apartment, she said, and the family soon moved out. Theresa said her mother then ordered her to set fire to the apartment; firefighters doused the blaze before it spread to the building's other four apartments...Theresa said she stayed with her mother for three years before running away at sixteen...

Inspector [Johnnie] Smith said Theresa's story is supported by statements from her brothers and by physical evidence found with the bodies. There are no plans to charge her, he said. She's married now, and officials are not releasing their key informant's new last name.

Theresa said she tried to tell her story starting in 1987, contacting an attorney and two police departments in Utah.

"The only thing that we can surmise is that the people she reported it to thought her story was so bizarre it couldn't be truthful," Smith said.[1]

Can you feel Theresa's pain? What is it like to forever hear the cries of your dying older sister? How long does the stench of rotting flesh remain in Theresa's memory? Who sees her tears? Is there anyone who understands?

Consider this thought by evangelist J. H. Jowett:

Does the cry of the world's need pierce the heart and ring even through the fabric of our dreams? I can take my newspaper, which is oftentimes a veritable cupful of horrors, and I can peruse it at the breakfast table, and it does not add a single tang to my feast. I wonder if one who is as unmoved can ever be a servant of the suffering Lord!...My brethren, I do not know how any Christian service is to be fruitful if the servant is not primarily baptized in the spirit of a suffering compassion.[2]

I wonder sometimes what it will take to wake us from our slumber. Does it have to be our child who is raped and killed at a major university? Must it be our father or mother who is sodomized by a nurse at a rest home? Must we receive the phone call that members of our family have just been massacred at a local fast-food restaurant? Do we wait until our child is molested at a day care center before we pick up the burden of the Lord? What will it take to affect us?

Perhaps you've noticed how the directors of many of our national programs are actual victims of the cause they're fighting. Sadly, that seems to be what it takes for many Christians to wake up. But it doesn't have to be that way.

Pick up any newspaper. Turn to any newscast. Theresa's mother and brothers are just actors on stage in a play that's gone mad. The scripts have been ripped up and thrown out; anything goes. We try to understand; we probe into the depths of a man's heart; we search until we're sick; and we come up empty.

This must be what Paul was speaking of when he wrote about the "mystery of lawlessness." "For the mystery of lawlessness is already at work" (2 Thess. 2:7). Mysteries are hard to figure out; they're an enigma. And the fact is, we live surrounded in a shroud of unsolved mysteries. Why do men do what they do and then cover it up? There is no fear of God before their eyes.

I'd like to tell you about a graphic dream I was given from the Lord. I cannot apologize for the next few pages, I have written the story just as it came to me, in vivid detail. Tears gushed from my eyes as the reality of it cut like a knife. I was seeing a distinct picture of the church, and now I am responsible for sharing it.

I was standing inside the front door of a business establishment. Within the confines of the room were about twenty-five employees: men and women, a variety of people, working hard, all doing their respective duties.

This particular business was extremely busy. The phone was constantly ringing, and a steady stream of people came and went. Everyone was diligently working away at a job when suddenly the door swung open.

There, standing in the doorway, was a huge, towering man, over seven feet tall. He stepped inside and stood like a statue at the entrance. No one noticed.

Looking into his eyes was like staring face-to-face into death. He looked straight at me but didn't flinch. I knew at that moment I was only in the room as a witness, unable to do anything. He looked at me fiercely, streetwise. From his hardened face came a frozen stare that will remain forever imprinted on my mind. He was angry.

He stood motionless. His fiery eyes roamed the room as if he were seeking out a familiar face — someone to burn. Then the horror began. He raised his left foot into the air and slammed it to the ground. The floor shook. Nobody moved. I stood in shock as the employees took no notice.

Then he raised his right foot, slammed it to the ground and again shook the floor. Still oblivious to the announcement of his arrival, the employees continued their duties.

In this man's left hand was a paper sack. Reaching in, he pulled out a bottle of whiskey. He raised the vial over his head and soaked his face. Within seconds his entire head was covered in the liquor. It filled his mouth and overflowed, pouring down his chin. His forehead was doused, obviously blurring his vision, as the burning alcohol flowed over his eyes.

With the bottle drained, he began shaking his head violently back and forth, his long stringy hair soaked in venom, whipping the air, slinging the whiskey everywhere. Nobody noticed; nobody moved.

Then he reached into his left pocket and pulled out a large, silver butcher knife. The blade glistened as he raised it over his head. With his eyes still roaming the room he let out a scream that pierced the air. The deadening cry shook the building. Finally, he got the people's attention.

The employees looked up and immediately were mortified. They stood motionless as if paralyzed by his presence. He raced over to the nearest woman, threw her to the ground, put the knife to her throat and screamed, "If anybody moves, she's dead." Then he raped her.

The man eyed one of the male employees. The worker was a large hulk of a man, but he stood frightened like a child. The giant man grabbed him, threw him face down to the ground and warned, "If anybody moves, I'll cut his throat." He sodomized him. The other employees stood in shame, hanging their heads.

Then the man went to the next woman and raped her. Then to the next man. The nightmare continued until half of the people had been abused. The other half stood motionless — and weeping. This can't be happening! Those who had been raped wallowed on the floor, groaning like abused animals.

The man was totally unaware of my presence, so I seized the moment and slipped out the front door. Within a few minutes I arrived with a SWAT team from the local police force. I'll never forget what took place.

The business had become a battlefield. On the floor were a dozen victims of war. Standing around were a dozen more, suffering from shock. No one was dead, but everyone was grieving. The faces spoke of deep emotional trauma. The grown men looked like scared little children, huddled together.

The head of the SWAT team screamed out, "Hey, you! Stop! Put down your weapon!" To my astonishment, the beast of a man swung around, his arms went limp and his fiery demeanor softened. Within seconds the atmosphere changed. Folding his hands behind his back, the SWAT team cuffed him and led him out. There was no fight, only absolute surrender. The violent saga was over.

I stepped out to the squad car to gain one last glimpse of the man who had wreaked havoc upon so many innocent lives. He looked my way, and our eyes met. His stare pierced my soul. Then he let out the most hideous laugh, as if to say, "I've had my fun and nobody could stop me. Now look at them. They can't even get off the floor. They're bleeding and dying in shame."

My wife remained motionless after I first related the dream to her. My own spirit was shaken. I knew there must be an interpretation. Jeri said she would pray, and I went to my prayer closet to pursue the Lord.

I wanted an answer. Alone in my secret place, where God had spoken so many times before, I waited for the interpretation. With a small tape recorder in hand, I prayed, "Jesus, I know You have just spoken, but I don't fully understand why. Please speak, Lord. Give me the full story. I want to understand it clearly, that I might know what Your Spirit is saying to the church."

The answer came. The Lord said, "Steve, the business that you were in is what everyone perceives as My church. You were inside the building to view the scene — that's why no one took notice of your presence. The activity of the employees represents the busyness of the ministry. Everyone is captivated in his or her own little world. Monotony has set in. They live as if hypnotized by the routine of Christian life. The tall, husky man who stepped in was Satan, the strong man."

Then my questions began. "Why the front door, Lord? Why not the back? We've always been taught that the devil slips in through the back door." The Lord answered, "He has come in through the front door and planted his feet firmly within the church. Throughout the centuries he has worked from without and from within. He is now firmly planted within." What did the slamming of his feet represent?

"When the sound of his feet thundered through the building, that represented many great devastations that have occurred within the church over the last several years. The enemy has made a lot of noise. The shaking, the danger, should have been obvious to all. Yet no one really took notice. No one changed."

The details unraveled precisely as the events had come in the dream. The bottle of whiskey, raised over his head and poured out, signified the outpouring of filth in these last days. The slinging of the poisonous liquid represented the saturation of evil. Everyone will be affected. As the interpretation unfolded, I thought of the Scripture, "In whom the god of this world hath blinded the minds of them which believe not" (2 Cor. 4:4, KJV). His liquid has splattered their eyes! The pouring out of the whiskey in his eyes, his mouth and all over his head signified the evil being totally out of control.

Few would deny that we are experiencing an outpouring of evil in the latter part of this century such as the world has rarely seen. No country has been exempt from Satan's hideous, vile atrocities. Yet in the midst of this baptism of filth, we still deny God.

The shiny, silver butcher knife signified Satan's weaponry. It is not only sharp but skillfully used. The raising of the knife over his head for all to see represents how the devil is blatant in many of his ways, yet no one notices. The church is not aware of his devices!

He has slipped in as an angel of light and stalks around as an angel of death. He has come in as a teacher of truth and twisted our minds as the father of lies. He has put his friendly arm around believers and within minutes cut them up like a fiend. He has promised light, laughter and life, but delivered darkness, depression and death.

Then there was the scream. This was the war cry of the enemy. He has unleashed every weapon. His army has been ordered to steal, kill and destroy. This is war!

But what about the rape and the sodomy, Lord? Why such horrendous acts of sexual perversion? Why such pain and humiliation?

The answer came clearly: "The act of rape is the most humiliating thing that can happen to a man or a woman. Consider the spiritual men who were once great soldiers of Mine. In the spiritual realm they have been sodomized — thrown to the ground, face down in the dirt, abused. They seemed defenseless under the enemy's grip and threats. They've been totally destroyed. Their ministry is over — they can't even get up. Many were choice servants of Mine. They did not recognize his entrance, didn't hear his war cry, lived totally oblivious to his actions. In the end, they fell to his cunning maneuvers."

Finally, I asked about the SWAT team.

"These are the righteous men and women of God. These are My

remnant. They are the ones who blow the trumpet in Zion, who have not bowed their knees to Baal. They have power over the enemy in the name of Jesus."

It all became so clear to me — crystal clear. The strong man had given up without a fight because he knew who this team represented! "Greater is He who is in you than he that is in the world" (1 John 4:4). The Lord has a people who know how to fight. They recognize the enemy and take him captive in the authority of God's name.

Now let's merge the stories and the dream. Sinners have been snared in a web of wickedness. They're sinking in a dark sea of damnation. They're waking up screaming, gasping for breath, in the middle of the night: "Somebody help me, I'm drowning!" Lies have engulfed them. They have swallowed gallons of contaminated water. Everything from traditional religion — with its rules, self-help books and three-step solutions — to the poison spewed out over the airwaves has sapped the strength of the unbelievers.

Exhausted from trying to swim, they begin to give up. It's no use, and they go down for the third time. Their hands violently slap the surface, trying to gain them just one more breath. They're choking; everything's a blur. Blindness begins to set in.

Then just as all hope has vanished, their blurred, bloodshot eyes focus on a passing ship. Could it be? God has heard their cry! "Help!" they scream. "Throw out a lifeline! I'm dying!" but they cry in vain.

Can you hear Sheila's suffocating cries from behind closed doors? Before her fatal captivity, her face spoke volumes about the destruction and death she'd seen, but nobody noticed. She had been deteriorating long before entering her closet-tomb.

Sadly, tragically, the cries from the dark fall on deaf ears. Why? Because here we find the saints being tossed about on an ocean of hype! Their condition is worse than that of the sinking sinner. They're too sick to save, so how can they throw out a lifeline? They lie face-down on the deck of their cruise ship. They can't even stand up. Buckled over with agonizing stomach cramps, they too plead for help. The hellish heaving seems endless.

They have come to this horrible condition because they have drunk from poisoned watering holes and eaten the meat of demons. Their life is as unstable as water, and they're being tossed about by every wind and wave of doctrine. The saints are seasick, nauseated from the noise. They want to help, but they can't move. Their body is rejecting not only the food but the ungodly feeder. Finally, they lean over the edge and spew up undigested, contaminated meat on the sea of life.

Unsuspecting unbelievers below are splattered with the falling filth. Those clamoring for a life preserver get slapped with vomit instead.

Who's that clamoring for help over there? Is that Mrs. Cross as a teenager? The murdering mother was once a troubled teen. She's crying for a lifeline, but nobody hears.

The smell of the sickness has permeated the nostrils of the ungodly, and now they flee from its stench. "Get out of here — and take your God with you! If this is what He does to you, then I'll have nothing to do with Him!"

This is no dream — it is real. Most Christians are unable to come to the aid of dying sinners because they are rocking and reeling in a nightmare of their own.

I am reminded of an inspirational conversation I had on a recent flight to Moscow. The topic of Bible study arose, and I began explaining my method of studying God's Word and how it has come alive to me.

Out of the blue spoke a man with this snobbish statement: "You will never understand God's Word unless you fully comprehend Greek and Hebrew. The English Bible is not an accurate interpretation of the Word of God."

This brother obviously was out of order, having entered our conversation without an invitation. I couldn't help it — my look to him was one of disgust. My mind raced to the hundreds of Christians I've met who claim all knowledge but have never come to a knowledge of the truth. They say they have a grip on the power of God's Word, but they've never prayed for someone to be healed. They claim to know the five techniques of evangelism, but they haven't personally led someone to the Lord in years. They are experts on prayer but are prayerless. They claim to know the Lord but seem powerless when confronted by the demon-possessed. They spend a lifetime agonizing over every doctrine and Bible translation when the whole world could be saved by hearing John 3:16 in any version.

In conclusion, we all must answer God's call, and when we do, we must strike the balance. With one ear we must hear the sweet music of heaven; with the other, the moans of hell. While we adoringly sing, "I've Got a Mansion," we must not forget also to sing, "Come and Go With Me to My Father's House."

William Booth, founder of The Salvation Army, summed it up well when he instructed:

> Nurse your people. I don't mean you should cozen and comfort and encourage the old do-nothing members...No! Tip up their cradle! Make them understand that true godliness is practical benevolence, and that they must at once become followers of Jesus, and go in for a life of self-sacrifice in order to do good and save souls, or else give up all hope and title to being Christians.[3]

My prayer is for every sleepy believer to feel the cradle tipping. We need to wake up and weep. We need to see through our Father's eyes. He will wean us from our whimpering and whining. He will give us something to cry about.

SEVEN

WEEPING THROUGH
THE WORD

The Bible was written in tears and
to tears it will yield its best treasure.
God has nothing to say to the frivolous man.
— A. W. Tozer

Mark Twain said, "Most people are bothered by those passages of Scripture they do not understand, but the passages that bother
me are those I do understand."[1]

Indeed, the Bible is crystal clear on the subject of crying. The Bible
reveals at least seven basic causes for weeping. It contains more than
seven hundred references to weeping, crying, tears and mourning.
Due to the enormity of data, I have categorized this chapter into seven
sections, each detailing with one type or cause of crying in the Scripture. I believe these are important to know, for when we rightly
interpret the source of this fountain of tears, we unveil the mysteries
of the soul.

Jesus, on His resurrection day, asked Mary a very exacting question. Standing beside her at the tomb, He said, "Woman, why are you
weeping?" (John 20:15). We too must learn to ask this question while
people are weeping at the tomb of a religious experience. And we must
listen to these weepers and answer according to their tearful responses.

Before listing the seven types or causes of weeping found in the Bible, I want to note five reasons for the tears shed by men, women and children in our evangelistic meetings. These five reasons are:

1. Overwhelming guilt is felt by people over their sinful condition as brought to light by the presence of Jesus Christ.

2. Overwhelming joy is felt as they are embraced by their heavenly Father. Tears flow as they experience His tender love and mercy, His peace which passes all understanding and the deep inner witness that He has everything under control.

3. Their present practices and indulgences have led them to a point of total abasement, and they find themselves destitute, at rock bottom.

4. They feel a gut conviction that they have wasted their lives and grieved the Lord, and now they desire to make things right regardless of the cost.

5. They come to the devastating realization that one day they will find themselves at the great Judgment and be cast into hell.

As we have preached the truth to audiences worldwide, we have seen everything from weeping warriors to sobbing stoics. Preaching the tear-stained Word of God pierces the innermost part of man and brings to reality the truth of his spiritual state. It has been said that God's Word is His personal love letter to Christians; I would add that it is also a tearful telegram to the wayward warrior, a fervent fax to those who are failing or fallen.

The solemn truth is, we are called to cry. The prophet Isaiah drives home this powerful point: "Therefore in that day the Lord God of hosts called you to weeping, to wailing, to shaving the head, and to wearing sackcloth. Instead, there is gaiety and gladness" (Is. 22:12).

The Lord commands us to "rejoice with those who rejoice, and weep with those who weep" (Rom. 12:15). There are times when we should be as the towering oaks of Bashan, boldly withstanding the forces of nature. Yet at other times we should be as the weeping willows by the rivers of Babylon, allowing our branches to humbly hang to the ground.

George Gilfillan, in his book *The Bards of the Bible,* shares his thoughts on the variety of weepers in the Word:

> Paul's tears effected what his thunders, his learning and his logic would not so quickly have done. Great as the difference between man and man, is that between tear and tear. The tears of Isaiah must have been fiery and rainbow-beaming as his genius; David's must have been mingled with blood; Jeremiah's must have been copious and soft as a woman's; Ezekiel's must have been wild and terrible tears. Of those of Jesus, what can we say, save that the glory of His greatness and the mildness of His meek humanity must have met in every drop. And Paul's, doubtless, were slow, quiet and large, as his profound nature. A Paul, too proud for tears, would have never turned the world upside down. We must mark the kindliness of that heart which lay below the sunlike splendor of his genius.[2]

WEEPING IN THE WORD

Now let's examine the seven references of weeping found in the Word. Keep in mind that this is just the beginning of an exploration into Scripture on the subject. By no means do I intend for the next few pages to be exhaustive.

1. REMEMBERING DAYS OF OLD

"By the rivers of Babylon, there we sat down and wept, when we remembered Zion. Upon the willows in the midst of it we hung our harps. For there our captors demanded of us songs, and our tormentors mirth, saying, 'Sing us one of the songs of Zion.' How can we sing the Lord's song in a foreign land?" (Ps. 137:1-4).

In this passage we find the transplanted Hebrews meditating on the wonders of the Lord. They once lived joyously in the beauty of their homeland. They remembered sipping on the fruit of the vine while relaxing under a shade tree. Their grateful hearts gave way to sweet songs of heaven. With their harps they glorified God, and with their lips they gave Him praise. But now the tune has changed. They have found themselves surrounded by the enemy in a strange land. Seated by the rivers of Babylon, they are asked by their captors to sing a melody, but they are unable to sing. "How can we sing the Lord's song in a foreign land?" they mournfully reply.

I remember many conversations with backslidden Christians before I gave my life to the Lord. Oftentimes while we were in a drunken stupor, the subject of Christianity came up. As we mused on the joys of the "pure life," tears fell from the backslider's eyes. On several occasions, I recall them saying something like, "I remember what it was like to go to sleep with peace in my heart. You don't know what it is to sing and worship with a clean conscience. Don't talk bad about Jesus. I used to live for Him, and it was wonderful."

But before the sin-sickened saint would start singing the blues, I would quickly change the subject, urging him to drown out his sorrow with another swig of beer. How could I expect him to sing the Lord's song while he lived the life of a captive?

One classic story concerning this sin-sick condition is found in Numbers 11. Here we read of the wandering children of Israel. You may be familiar with the details of this story. The children of Israel seemed to be blinded while in the midst of an incredible deliverance. They groaned while scooping up manna from the ground. Nothing would satisfy them; they cried like colicky babies. So God's anger was kindled toward them, and their griping and complaining brought down His fire from heaven.

"What am I to do?" cried Moses, their righteous leader. "They weep before me!" Moses took it all personally:

> Why hast Thou been so hard on Thy servant? And why have I not found favor in Thy sight, that Thou hast laid the burden of all this people on me? Was it I who conceived all this people? Was it I who brought them forth, that Thou shouldest say to me, "Carry them in your bosom as a nurse carries a nursing infant, to the land which Thou didst swear to their fathers?" Where am I to get meat to give to all this people? For they weep before me, saying "Give us meat that we may eat!" I alone am not able to carry all this people, because it is too burdensome for me. So if Thou art going to deal thus with me, please kill me at once, if I have found favor in Thy sight, and do not let me see my wretchedness (Num. 11:11-15).

Over the centuries, how many faithful servants of the Lord have cried out as Moses did? How many godly pastors have done everything possible to help their congregation, only to find themselves wallowing in the muck and mire of the people's murmuring?

Well the Hebrews got their meat! According to historians, the least amount gathered by each person was ten homers, or over 450 gallons (v. 32). Their rebellion led to greediness, their greediness to overindulgence, their overindulgence to death. So it is today when we act as squalling, blubbering babies through our seasons of suffering.

Death, despair and depression led the children of Israel into fits of rebellion. The desert sun had blinded their eyes. They cried and complained over their lost lifestyle in Egypt. And so it is today for many Christians. Satan places a mesmerizing mirage before our eyes during our desert trial. We see clearly the carnal delights of years gone by while he so craftily omits the sufferings of slavery. We are convinced that those were the good old days. Our tears begin to fall as we remember back nostalgically.

So many of us stand at the crossroads begging for a spiritual handout. We used to be on fire for God, but now lukewarmness has set in. Our saddened countenance speaks of poverty and despair but underneath is deceit and slothfulness. All we really want is a quick fix. When our pastor walks by, we shake our tin cup. In disgust, he tosses in another gospel truth and wonders when this poor beggar will get up and work. "What more does God have to do for you?" he angrily mumbles to himself. He knows we are street urchins, complacently looking to a man for a morsel of food when God has prepared a feast!

When will we quit complaining, wipe away our baby tears and face the music? When will we drop the tin cup and go on with God? All our fussing and fuming will bring out the same Father quality in God that fell on the children of Israel. They wanted a feast and kindled a fire; their murmuring turned to mourning. As the English commentator Matthew Henry said, "It is not poverty, but discontent that makes a man unhappy."

The psalmist David moaned before the Lord: "Be gracious to me, O Lord, for I am in distress; My eye is wasted away from grief, my soul and my body also. For my life is spent with sorrow, and my years with sighing; my strength has failed because of my iniquity, and my body wasted away" (Ps. 31:9-10). David knew what it was to compare his present dilemma with his past delights. He once walked in the joy of the Lord, but later he wallowed in wickedness. Tears were his language.

Peter shed bitter tears when the shocking reality of his sin hit home. "And immediately a cock crowed a second time. And Peter remembered how Jesus had made the remark to him, 'Before a cock crows twice, you will deny Me three times'" (Mark 14:72). "I have betrayed my Lord," he mourned. He went out and wept bitterly. These are the tears when we remember the days of old. And it is while in our rebellious, backslidden condition that we remember God. "I remembered God, and was troubled," confesses the psalmist (Ps. 77:3, KJV).

2. AT A PLACE OF TOTAL ABASEMENT

This is the valley of Baca — literally, "the valley of weeping" (see Ps. 84:6). It is the place of spiritual drought we've all passed through. It was probably an allegorical name given to an experience rather than an actual location, much like the valley of the shadow of death. Yet regardless, our well has run dry, and our tongue is parched. We are destitute, longing for a spiritual oasis: "Blessed is the man whose strength is in thee; in whose heart are the ways of them. Who passing through the valley of Baca make it a well; the rain also filleth the pools" (Ps. 84:5-6, KJV).

This is a place in our spiritual lives of total abasement. It is when we're scraping bottom; when the world's pressure is clamping down from all sides; when ministry's pains come crashing in; when if God doesn't move, there will be no more moving.

The cry is deep, emotional, desperate and sincere. It is motivated by a gut belief in Jesus, regardless of the circumstances. "Help, Jesus! Lift me up!" Tears flow like a river. "Dear Lord, if You don't reach down and pick me up, it's over." It is the cry of an agonizing man, the groanings of a weary pilgrim, the strainings of a sinking soul. It is the cry for life!

Mary,* a friend, was raised in a violent, alcoholic home. She remembers such a time of spiritual depravity. "I had lost all hope, self-esteem and ambition," she testified. "Bitterness and anger grew as the months slipped into years. Then in my rebellious condition, my husband took me to church. I cried during each service and could not explain why. Tears clouded my eyes and drenched my face. It was there God began healing the wounds and setting me free."

For most of us, David comes to mind when we speak of tearful repentance. He writes: "I am weary with my sighing; Every night I

*Not her real name

make my bed swim, I dissolve my couch with my tears. My eye has wasted away with grief; It has become old because of all my adversaries. Depart from me, all you who do iniquity, for the Lord has heard the voice of my weeping" (Ps. 6:6-8).

These are the times of a salty diet of tears. The psalmist said, "My tears have been my food day and night" (Ps. 42:3). Indeed, tears are the bread of mourners.

Such tender times together with Jesus are often flooded with tears of repentance. These, in turn, are followed by tears of exaltation and then by tears of joy. The stream of tears bubbles from Genesis to Revelation, at times swelling into a mighty river.

In Psalm 107 we hear God's people bemoaning their peril and crying out to the Lord for deliverance. The words are similar to those of the patriarch Job: "My face is flushed from weeping, and deep darkness is on my eyelids, although there is no violence in my hands, and my prayer is pure" (Job 16:16-17).

When Job spoke those words, he was in the valley of the shadow of death. And it is here also that we find Hosea weeping and pleading to the Lord: "He wept, and made supplication unto him" (Hos. 12:4, KJV).

Huldah, the prophetess, speaks words of comfort to those in this place of total abasement: "'Because your heart was tender and you humbled yourself before God, when you heard His words against this place and against its inhabitants, and because you humbled yourself before Me, tore your clothes, and wept before Me, I truly have heard you,' declares the Lord" (2 Chr. 34:27).

3. WHEN THE ENEMY HAS TRIUMPHED

"But if you will not listen to it, My soul will sob in secret for such pride; and my eyes will bitterly weep and flow down with tears, because the flock of the Lord has been taken captive" (Jer. 13:17).

During such times, God's command is clear: "Awake, drunkards, and weep; and wail, all you wine drinkers, on account of the sweet wine that is cut off from your mouth" (Joel 1:5).

"For these things I weep; My eyes run down with water; Because far from me is a comforter, One who restores my soul; My children are desolate because the enemy has prevailed" (Lam. 1:16).

Nobody likes to lose. I recently spoke to a Fellowship of Christian Athletes high school group in Ohio. The Lord had laid upon my heart this very subject: "We are losing." That particular high school had more than two thousand students, and only a small percentage were believers. Several of the Christian athletes at the meeting were broken by the fact that God's winning team was actually sitting on the sidelines letting the enemy run rampant down the field. "Where is God's army?" I asked. "Where is our awesome God? Who is storming the gates of hell?'"

The brokenness that followed led many of those young soldiers to the front lines of battle. One later testified of incredible victories as he began sharing the gospel with his unsaved friends.

The Bible says, "Then all the sons of Israel and all the people went up and came to Bethel and wept...they fasted...and offered burnt offerings" (Judg. 20:26). Bethel signifies the house of God, where God dwells. During these times of apparent defeat we must get close to God; we must press on. Our river of tears must lead us to the harbor of His will.

As David did, upon gazing at the destruction left behind by the Amalekites, we too must lift up our voices and weep, until there is no more power to weep (see 1 Sam. 30:1-8). After a good cry, we must get up and fight. We must set our affections on things above. Our goals must become God's goals. Our possessions must become tools, not traps. Most of all, our desires must become His.

Nehemiah was moved to mourning over the devastation of Jerusalem. "And they said to me, 'The remnant in the province who survived the captivity are in great distress and reproach, and the wall of Jerusalem is broken down and its gates are burned with fire'" (Neh. 1:3). Nehemiah responded correctly to the tragic news: "Now it came about when I heard these words, I sat down and wept and mourned for days; and I was fasting and praying before the God of heaven" (v. 4).

There is a time to weep, just as surely as there is a time to laugh. We often hear Nehemiah's proclamation today: "The church has been reproached! Many walls of protection have fallen, and the fires of hell are blazing within!" These are times to break before God and bemoan the devastation of the land. "Therefore I will weep bitterly for Jazer, for the vine of Sibmah; I will drench you with my tears, O Heshbon and Elealeh; For the shouting over your summer fruits and your harvest has fallen away" (Is. 16:9).

"More than the weeping for Jazer I shall weep for you, O vine of Sibmah! Your tendrils stretched across the sea, they reached to the sea of Jazer; Upon your summer fruits and your grape harvest the destroyer has fallen" (Jer. 48:32). "Behold their brave men cry in the streets, the ambassadors of peace weep bitterly" (Is. 33:7).

We must tearfully turn back to God! As we gaze upon the loveliness of Christ — as we meditate on His beauty, His purpose, His plan — we must do as the psalmist and muse on all His wonderful deeds of old (see Ps. 77:11-12). And the things of this earth — the trappings, the chains, the bondages — will all fall away.

The further we are from Christ, the more earthly we become, and we begin losing the battle of life. Rather than being pilgrims who are passing through, we plant ourselves deep in the soil of this present world. Our affections, goals and desires are earth-formed and earth-bound. We become tied down to a passing reality. Soon we realize, as the prodigal did, that it is all a mirage. In this world there is nothing to grab hold of, nothing eternal — all is empty.

We do well to remember the innocence of our first days with Jesus. It was a time when nothing mattered but the simplicity of living holy and winning people to Him. After all, aren't those the two most important things? Doesn't everything else fall under these two categories? But oh, how we've complicated our lives!

"Get back to God!" scream the prophets. "Therefore I say, 'Turn your eyes away from me, let me weep bitterly, do not try to comfort me concerning the destruction of the daughter of my people' " (Is. 22:4). Isaiah was crying, "Don't wipe my eyes, don't even look my way. Weep, wail, cry out to the Lord yourself over the devastating destruction of sin. Look what we've done with our lives!" What deep concern, what travailing. "Oh, that my head were waters, and my eyes a fountain of tears, that I might weep day and night for the slain of the daughter of my people!" (Jer. 9:1).

The prophet Joel joins into this chorus of tears, exhorting each and every minister to fall on his face before the Lord:

> Let the priests, the Lord's ministers, weep between the porch and the altar, and let them say, "Spare Thy people, O Lord, and do not make Thine inheritance a reproach, a byword among the nations. Why should they among the peoples say, 'Where is their God?'" (Joel 2:17).

All our weeping must initiate a response. We want God to respond and help us. He wants us to respond by taking action.

Now while Ezra was praying and making confession, weeping and prostrating himself before the house of God, a very large assembly, men, women, and children, gathered to him from Israel; for the people wept bitterly. And Shecaniah the son of Jehiel, one of the sons of Elam, answered and said to Ezra, "We have been unfaithful to our God, and have married foreign women from the peoples of the land; yet now there is hope for Israel in spite of this" (Ezra 10:1-2).

The brokenness must lead to action on the part of God's people. Ezra's command rings through the ages: "Arise! For this matter is your responsibility, but we will be with you; be courageous and act" (Ezra 10:4).

4. WHEN THE LORD WEPT

What causes a king to cry? What is it we do that causes grief enough to produce tears on the face of our Father? Benjamin Beddome wrote:

> Did Christ o'er sinners weep,
> And shall our cheeks be dry?
> Let floods of penitential grief
> Burst forth from every eye.
>
> The Son of God in tears
> The wondering angels see!
> Be thou astonished, O my soul:
> He shed those tears for thee.

The Scriptures record three moments when our Lord's emotions surfaced through tears. The most memorable is well-known as the shortest verse in the Bible. This was over the death of His friend Lazarus: "Jesus wept" (literally, shed tears; John 11:35). His open display of emotion caused those nearby to exclaim, "Oh, how He loved him."

It is important for us to read this verse in context. You see, the previous verse tells us why Jesus wept. "When Jesus therefore saw her weeping, and the Jews who came with her, also weeping, He was deeply moved in spirit, and was troubled" (v. 33).

It is interesting to note that Jesus had said to the widow of Nain at the funeral of her only son, "Weep not" (Luke 7:13, KJV). And, to those bereaved of the daughter of Jairus, He said, "Why make ye this ado, and weep?" (Mark 5:39, KJV). Yet we see here that Jesus moaned and shed tears at the death of His own good friend. This is a picture to us of the depth of the humanity of our Savior. He felt every emotion and experienced personally the depth of every earthly trial.

On another occasion — after His incredible triumphal entry into Jerusalem — He stood upon the hill and wept over the city's eminent destruction. What motivated the Son of God to mourn over Jerusalem?

Luke 19:41 says Jesus saw the city and wept over it. The original text expresses "loud cries."[4] His wailing was warranted. You see, Jesus saw everything through the eyes of eternity. His compassion was intermingled with eternal tears, and when the Lord wept, He always took action.

Whenever we hear the word compassion mentioned, most of us consider the present plight of man — man's suffering; the agony of survival on this planet; the lack of food, clothing and shelter; the unjust distribution of the world's goods; the beggar at the foot of the rich man's gate; the starving child scraping every last morsel from his tray; the homeless, on a cold winter night, under a bridge, huddled around a blazing fire; the runaway teenager, weeping as she wanders.

Although these needs are for the most part legitimate, there is more to weep over — much, much more. Jesus saw far beyond the present troubles. Our present conditions have to do with the temporal, not the eternal. Although one flows into the other, the latter carries inexpressible importance. After all, what does it profit a man if he gains the whole world and loses his own soul? What good is it if a man receives another pair of shoes to walk on this earth, when in a flash he'll stand naked and barefoot at the judgment? What sense does it make for him to fill his belly when his heart is empty? Why shelter a man from the wiles of this present age, when all the demons of hell are penetrating his unguarded soul? We spend billions protecting ourselves from the predators without while we neglect the predators within!

True compassion has eternity in focus. Jesus' tears were not as Hezekiah's when the king wept over his fatal sickness (2 Kin. 20:1-3) — those tears were temporal. The tears of our Lord had to do with eternity, for He sees the future. He knew that the very ones who were praising Him today would be crying out, "Crucify Him!" tomorrow.

So Jesus wept eternal tears over Jerusalem. When He gazed at Jerusalem from the lofty hillside, the scene was overwhelming. He knew that soon He would be gazing down from another hill, Golgotha. Thoughts flooded His mind. He was standing on the edge of the city which would be devastated by war within a generation. He saw the tenth Roman legion marching in, making camp and turning the city to rubble. Knowing the future as He did, His heart was filled with indescribable sadness. Tears welled up from deep within. Jerusalem was lost — those in darkness again rejected the light.

It was in this frame of mind that He said to the weeping women on the road to Golgotha, "Daughters of Jerusalem, stop weeping for Me, but weep for yourselves and for your children" (Luke 23:28). Knowing the future — certain destruction — He was no longer able to withhold His anguish. His humanity was deeply moved. Tears burst from His eyes as He saw the destruction. The walls were coming down; men and women would be slaughtered; their homes looted; all that had been gained, lost. What does it profit a man?

Just as Jesus fixed His eyes on eternity, so should we in our pilgrimage. Every person we meet, every cup of water we give, every grain of wheat we distribute should be directly connected to the person's soul.

The third mention of Jesus' tears is found in Hebrews 5:7: "In the days of His flesh, He offered up prayers with loud crying and tears to One able to save Him from death." Our thoughts race to Gethsemane when we think of this portion of Scripture, but I think it had more to do with Jesus' entire life. I can imagine that during His quiet times alone with the Father, His sobbing was done in secret. During these blessed times, the humanity of God's only Son surfaced: He was a man of sorrows, acquainted with grief. He knew that the only comfort was to be found bathing the feet of His heavenly Father with tears.

5. EMOTION EMANATING FROM DEEP CONCERN, WORSHIP OR PRAYER

Listen to Isaiah: "Like a swallow, like a crane, so I twitter; I moan like a dove; My eyes look wistfully to the heights; O Lord, I am oppressed, be my security" (Is. 38:14).

Rachel joins in this crying chorus: "A voice was heard in Ramah, weeping and great mourning, Rachel weeping for her children; and she refused to be comforted, because they were no more" (Matt. 2:18).

The harmony continues in the Psalms: "Hear my prayer, O Lord!

And let my cry for help come to Thee...For I have eaten ashes like bread, and mingled my drink with weeping" (Ps. 102:1,9).

Indeed, the emotional tears throughout the centuries flow together, forming a mighty river to heaven. We find the tears of Joseph upon meeting his brothers: "And Joseph hurried out for he was deeply stirred over his brother, and he sought a place to weep; and he entered his chamber and wept there" (Gen. 43:30).

We find the tears of Paul, shed for his beloved children at Philippi: "For many walk, of whom I often told you, and now tell you even weeping, that they are enemies of the cross of Christ" (Phil. 3:18). And again Paul sheds tears over his children in Corinth: "For out of much affliction and anguish of heart I wrote to you with many tears; not that you should be made sorrowful, but that you might know the love which I have especially for you" (2 Cor. 2:4). There is also his farewell address to the believers at Ephesus: "Therefore be on the alert, remembering that night and day for a period of three years I did not cease to admonish each one with tears" (Acts 20:31). Yes, Paul was a weeper.

Listen to Mary at the tomb of her Lord: "But Mary was standing outside the tomb weeping; and so, as she wept, she stooped and looked into the tomb...Jesus said to her, 'Woman, why are you weeping? Whom are you seeking?'" (John 20:11,15).

There is the act of tearful footbathing by the dear woman expressing her thankful heart: "And as she stood behind him at his feet weeping, she began to wet his feet with her tears. Then she wiped them with her hair, kissed them and poured perfume on them" (Luke 7:38, NIV).

Once again, Paul surfaces on this river of tears — only this time his followers are weeping. Shackled and on his way to an uncertain final destiny, Paul says, "'What are you doing, weeping and breaking my heart? For I am ready not only to be bound, but even to die at Jerusalem for the name of the Lord Jesus.' And since he would not be persuaded, we fell silent, remarking, 'The will of the Lord be done!'" (Acts 21:13-14).

Could you imagine the scene at the death of Aaron and then again at the funeral service of Moses? The Bible says, "All the house of Israel wept for Aaron thirty days" (Num. 20:29). "So the sons of Israel wept for Moses in the plains of Moab thirty days; then the days of weeping and mourning came to an end" (Deut. 34:8).

In the Word we also find Elkanah, the husband of Hannah, responding to his wife's tears: "Hannah, why do you weep and why do you not eat and why is your heart sad? Am I not better to you than ten sons?...And she, greatly distressed, prayed to the Lord and wept bitterly [literally, "bitterness of soul"]" (1 Sam. 1:8,10). We know the rest of the story: Her deep mourning was turned to dancing upon the birth of her son, Samuel.

Tears of joy were shed at the family reunion of Jacob and Esau. "Then Esau ran to meet him and embraced him, and fell on his neck and kissed him, and they wept" (Gen. 33:4).

The Bible also records great emotional weeping as the Word of God was read. "For all the people were weeping when they heard the words of the law" (Neh. 8:9).

The widow of Nain is found weeping beside the casket of her only son. Then Christ comes alongside her — the true Comforter arrives. To others, her tears were just ordinary expressions of grief. But to Jesus, they spoke of far deeper pain and misery. Perhaps He thought of what His own mother would soon experience on the day of His death. Maybe the book of Jeremiah came to mind: "Mourn as for an only son, a lamentation most bitter. For suddenly the destroyer will come upon us" (Jer. 6:26).

Or perhaps He saw the poor woman trying to "scrape out a living" by the sweat of her brow because her only son had died. Perhaps His heart remembered Zechariah speaking of the "mourning of Hadadrimmon": "And they shall look upon me whom they have pierced, and they shall mourn for him, as one mourneth for his only son, and shall be in bitterness for him, as one that is in bitterness for his firstborn. In that day shall there be a great mourning in Jerusalem, as the mourning of Hadadrimmon in the valley of Megiddon" (Zech. 12:10-11). Perhaps upon gazing at her tears, Jesus thought of the death of King Josiah over six hundred years before and of the national lamentation made for him.

In an instant He became overwhelmed with the desire to "stop the suffering." Once again, His compassion moved Him to action. Her pain was soon relieved by the resurrection of her only child — a mighty fulfillment of the holy mandate to weep with those who weep.

6. WEEPING AND GNASHING OF TEETH

Jesus spoke of the quenchless flame, the undying worm, the eternal unforgiveness, the body and soul plunged in Gehenna and the weeping and gnashing of teeth. Each of these were His attempts to build a fear of eternal damnation. The weeping and gnashing of teeth, in particular, denotes severe rage coupled with sorrow. The force of this warning — the eternal grinding of teeth and ceaseless crying — was intended to deter the hearers from this dreadful end. It's interesting that part of our heavenly reward will be no more weeping, while part of the curse of hell will be eternal weeping.

Consider these words of John Bunyan:

> O damned men! this is your fate;
> The day of grace is done;
> Repentance now doth come too late
> Mercy is fled and gone.
>
> Your groans and cries the sooner should
> Have sounded in Mine ears,
> If grace you would have had, or would
> Have Me regard your tears.
>
> Me you offended with your sin,
> Instructions you did slight;
> Your sins against My law hath been
> Justice shall have his right.
>
> I gave My Son to do you good,
> I gave you space and time
> With Him to close, which you withstood,
> And did with hell combine.
>
> Justice against you now is set,
> Which you cannot appease:
> Eternal Justice doth you let
> From either life or ease.
>
> Thus he that to this place doth come
> May groan, and sigh, and weep,
> But sin hath made that place his home,
> And there it will him keep.[5]

7. WHEN GOD SHALL WIPE AWAY OUR TEARS HERE ON EARTH AND WHEN CRYING WILL CEASE FOREVER IN HEAVEN

Have you ever wept upon hearing the words of the Lord? For some of us, nothing could have stopped the tears from flowing as the Word of God pierced our hearts.

But there is a time to weep and a time to rejoice. Once again, let's reflect on the emotional scene from the book of Nehemiah.

> Then Nehemiah, who was the governor, and Ezra the priest and scribe, and the Levites who taught the people said to all the people, "This day is holy to the Lord your God; do not mourn or weep." For all the people were weeping when they heard the words of the law. Then he said to them, "Go, eat of the fat, drink of the sweet, and send portions to him who has nothing prepared; for this day is holy to our Lord. Do not be grieved, for the joy of the Lord is your strength" (Neh. 8:9-10).

We can rejoice — for there is coming a time of restoration! God shall wipe all tears from our eyes.

> O people in Zion, inhabitants in Jerusalem, you will weep no longer. He will surely be gracious to you at the sound of your cry; when He hears it, He will answer you. Although the Lord has given you bread of privation and water of oppression, He, your Teacher will no longer hide Himself, but your eyes will behold your Teacher. And your ears will hear a word behind you, "This is the way, walk in it," whenever you turn to the right or to the left (Is. 30:19-21).

"And He shall wipe away every tear from their eyes; and there shall no longer be any death; there shall no longer be any mourning, or crying, or pain; the first things have passed away" (Rev. 21:4).

"I will wipe all tears from your eyes." He isn't talking about our senseless whining, our selfish sorrow that life isn't going our way, our blatant church bickering over the color of the carpet or the size of the seats. He's not wiping the tears of sulking saints. No, the tears spoken of here are legitimate, godly tears — tears that issue from human suffering. It's interesting to note that when John visited heaven during his revelation he wept because there was found no man worthy to open the book:

> And I saw in the right hand of Him that sat on the throne a

book written and on the back, sealed up with seven seals. And I saw a strong angel proclaiming with a loud voice, "Who is worthy to open the book and to break its seals?" And no one in heaven, or on the earth, or under the earth, was able to open the book or to look into it. And I began to weep greatly because no one was found worthy to open the book, or to look into it (Rev. 5:1-4).

I am startled at such a revelation; the fact that no one could be found to crack open the book is a mystery to me. What about the faithful martyrs? What about those dying in this century, all over the world, for the cause of Christ? What about the human torches lighting Nero's gardens by night? Surely their sufferings, their pain, their agony have ascended as sweet incense to heaven and merit the right to slip open the book.

Let's consider one such saint in particular: a beautiful child full of faith named Susanna. She's six years old. Her name signifies a lily, and she's as precious as a fresh morning flower — blonde hair, blue eyes, and in love with Jesus.

The year is A.D. 404, and Susanna's entire family has been chosen to entertain the wicked Roman emperor and a host of heathen. Within a few minutes Mom, Dad, little Jeremiah and Susanna will be dead.

The family has been given the opportunity to recant their faith in Christ. "Deny Him and live," they are told.

"Impossible," they humbly respond. "He is everything to us."

"Then you shall die as fools. Prove to us how much your love for Jesus means!" Susanna is first. Two brawny soldiers, clutching her tiny arms, hastily lead her away. In a cold, dingy room a stinking lambskin is stitched to her clothing. At a distance she has the appearance of a scared little animal. Upon closer examination, she is more frightened than words can express. Then she is led to the arena floor. The crowd roars its approval.

Who can bear to watch the scene unfold? There she is, in a sprawling stadium, all alone. Her parents turn their heads from the horror. Thousands watch in earthly approval below while a heavenly host watches from above. One waits above for her heavenly arrival.

The starving lions are released. The ravenous beasts haven't eaten for two days. Within seconds they spot their prey. Suddenly, like a torrential rain, fear floods the heart of little Susanna. *This is real! I'm all alone. Mommy and Daddy aren't here to help me. I'm going to be eaten by that lion.* Tears begin to fall.

One of the animals begins to charge, and the little girl is no match. Her right arm is ripped off as she tries to flee. The pain is unlike anything she's ever experienced. The roaring of the crowd drowns out her cries for help. She falls to the ground. The other starving killers move in. Like vises, their jaws clamp down. Within minutes it's over.

Who's next? They call for little Jeremy.

Surely these children are worthy to open the book. And surely John's desire to see it opened would be satisfied by the martyrdom of little Susanna.

What about dear John the Baptist? The man of God who lived on locusts and honey, crying out night and day, "Prepare ye the way of the Lord!" He gave his all to secure his calling, and he gained a following only to turn them over to the One whose sandal he wasn't worthy to unlatch. Surely his humility, his Christlikeness, his zeal for the Lord, his dedication unto death has placed him above all others. Surely God looked upon his severed head presented on a platter before a group of reveling heathen and said, "My beloved John the Baptist! He is the one; he can open the book." Not a chance.

The question is, "Who is worthy?" The answer, once again, is Jesus. The Lamb of God will turn the pages. Dry your eyes, dear apostle!

Yes, all our tears will be wiped away because He won. One day we will all be blessed with heavenly, dry-eye syndrome because He conquered the earthly, wet-eye syndrome.

In the words of Benjamin Beddome:

> He wept that we might weep;
> Each sin demands a tear:
> In heaven alone no sin is found,
> And there's no weeping there.[6]

Solomon's wisdom easily applies today: "It is better to go to a house of mourning than to go to a house of feasting, because that is the end of every man, and the living takes it to heart" (Eccl. 7:2).

Indeed, the Bible has over seven hundred references to weeping, crying, tears and mourning. When we rightly interpret the source of our fountain of tears, we begin to unveil the mysteries of the soul.

EIGHT

TRAVAILING TEARS

*We truly travail over others only
when we feel the effects of their suffering —
when we empathize and enter their misery.*

There's something wrong here. Dear Jesus, help me to see from Your point of view. I want to see through eternity's eyes. The Word of God says You will give me understanding in all things (1 Tim. 2:7). I ask You, Father, help me to understand what is going on!"

That was my prayer early one morning during a recent visit to the former Soviet Union. We had been received by the Russian people with warm enthusiasm. They were responding to our friendship and were tasting our gospel message. The famine for truth there was obvious. The altar call the night before had been breathtaking: People flocked to the cross, many with tears in their eyes.

I had preached on John 1:29, "Behold the Lamb of God, which taketh away the sin of the world" (KJV). What a sight we beheld! Scores of young people came to the Lord. We prayed with them, and they asked Jesus to be Lord and Savior of their lives. Many wept at the realization of their spiritual depravity.

Their testimonies were evidence that real changes were taking place. One teenager said the presence of God had become obvious to him. With a face that literally beamed hope, he confessed, "This is the first time I felt there was a God. Now I know He exists!" A teenage girl said her thoughts had changed since praying the night before. "When I went to bed I was thinking differently," she said, her face radiant with Christ's love. "I'm so happy, so free!"

That night we had been thrilled to see the smiling faces and hear the wonderful stories. But now, in the morning after, I awoke grieving in my spirit. Why?

The Lord seemed to be speaking a gentle warning to me: "Are they truly meeting Me, Steve? Do you really believe that all of these people are meeting Me? Or are many still confused? Are they actually tasting of My goodness? Or are they following you with their actions but not with their hearts? Will they continue walking with Me after you're gone? Or will they just chalk this up as another religious experience with the westerners? Be very careful — things are not always what they seem."

These questions plagued me. Were all the conversions we'd seen just another case of "religious fickleness"? Would I be repeating in a few months' time the words of Paul: "I marvel that ye are so soon removed" (Gal. 1:6, KJV). The Galatians received Paul as if he were an angel, yet they began falling away from the gospel almost as quickly as they came to Christ.

I began a self-examination. I've come to the point in my life when every work must be analyzed; each project must weather an intense cross-examination. As a dear friend once told me, "Be careful about your work, Steve. Make sure you're involved in what God has planned. If not, you might stand on judgment day knee-deep in ashes."

My inquiry continued. "Has travailing prayer given birth to these new believers; or is this all just another case of 'spiritual rape'?" I trembled at the thought of the possible answer. *Am I just another evangelist, one of hundreds who have gleaned the whitened fields of Russia? Are my few hours in prayer really bringing these eternal results? And will this fruit remain?*

I have learned that the true test of all evangelistic labor is, in a phrase, "ten years after." (That is the reason we have dedicated our ministry to church planting.) *Where will these people be ten years from now?* I thought. *Will they know God, or will their hearts be cold and hard? Has the love of God truly permeated them, or are we being deceived?*

Finally I had to admit that a deep, overpowering burden for the lost in Russia had never permeated my soul. I had not spent days upon days travailing in my spirit over the spiritual destiny of that darkened country.

The words of Mom Wilkerson, mother of evangelist David Wilkerson, rang true to me again. I recalled a time, years before, when she had taught a group of us about evangelism. Her years of experience as an evangelist seasoned her every word. We had been planning to take an evangelism trip to New York City, and she was exuberant once more at the thought of walking the streets of that sin-infested city.

At the conclusion of our session with her, one student blurted out the following confession: "But I don't have a burden for New York City."

I'll never forget Mom Wilkerson's blunt response: "That's because you've never walked the streets of New York. God will burden you when you get there."

I have seen this incredible truth driven home around the world. Upon arriving at a specific area of labor, we sense an overwhelming burden being placed on our shoulders. We walk, talk and sleep with the people on our minds. And soon our fastings and prayer give way to incredible spiritual encounters. Visits to people's homes are often emotional, leading to weeping and repentance. The burden is real!

Now, walking the streets of Russia, our team developed a God-placed burden for the people's souls. We were now feeling their lost condition and weeping sincere, Holy Ghost tears for their souls.

Yet the harvest we now saw happening in Russia was the direct result of decades of fastings and prayers — not by us, but by others who had travailed for years. Indeed, someone else had cried out, "Dear God, save my people. Melt their hearts. Break through the oppression, dear Jesus, and send Your light to this dark, desolate land." Some other saint had felt the birth pangs, those sharp, sudden spasms of pain. Someone else had experienced the sharp emotional distress, forcing out hot, travailing tears. Others before us had filled up bottles of liquid grief in the secret closet of prayer. They had entered into the emotional stress of the "war in the heavenlies." Other prayer warriors had wrestled, "not against flesh and blood but against principalities and powers," for the people of Russia.

Of course I had prayed, and so had our team. But none of us had truly travailed. Now, I must say, we felt the heat of the battle. But for us, it resulted in instant victory followed by overwhelming joy. Those who had gone before us most assuredly had fought for decades without any visible results. They had experienced true labor pains. Perhaps they'd even felt the horror of hopelessness — the fear of their child being stillborn.

Nevertheless, the truth rang out to us loud and clear: Someone else's labor was not in vain. Could it be that the verse, "Your toil is not in vain in the Lord" (1 Cor. 15:58), also includes spiritual labor — that is, the labor of spiritual childbirth?

William Jay, a distinguished, independent English minister of the late eighteenth century, said, "Many who are great in the sight of the Lord are living in cottages and hovels and are scarcely known, unless to a few neighbors equally obscure." I believe these are the ones who have travailed over Russia. I am convinced that the greatest prayer warriors — those who have felt the pains of childbirth — will rarely be applauded here on earth but will receive their due crown in heaven. They are the ones who have not aborted Russia. Like dedicated, expectant parents, they have "stuck with it" all the way to the end.

Our team in Russia would have agreed with the apostle Paul, who said, "I have planted, Apollos watered; but God gave the increase. So then neither is he that planteth any thing, neither he that watereth; but God that giveth the increase. Now he that planteth, and he that watereth are one: *and every man shall receive his own reward according to his own labor*" (1 Cor. 3:6-8, KJV, italics added).

In the case of Russia, we obviously were reaping where someone else had labored — a labor that was not one-on-one with man, but one-on-one with God. Although most of these new converts were hearing the gospel for the first time, I knew that some dear saints had wrestled with God for decades until this answer came. They had travailed over the hard spiritual ground, turned the soil, planted and tearfully watered — all in the dark of the night. They could only hope for a harvest and dream of a promised land. Now in the light of day, we came in to reap.

I was humbled when an elderly man approached me and said we were the answer to their fifty years of prayers. The words of Jesus spoke clearly that day: "I sent you to reap that for which you have not labored; others have labored, and you have entered into their labor" (John 4:38).

Now several months after the crusade, we rejoice at the reports coming in. Many of the converts had truly given their hearts to the

Lord, and they are now actively involved in the newly started local church. However, my suspicions turned out to be correct. One recent letter stated, "Many don't really believe what you said happened in your life and don't trust your words."[1]

Those words echo what I felt during that early morning in the solitude of my hotel room. People had been nodding in approval, some even praying with us, but they were not sincere. Now an ever-increasing burden is developing in my heart for those souls in Russia who still have doubts.

There have been many occasions when God has placed a burden on my heart for someone in peril. Not long ago I was overwhelmed by a spiritual attack on some good friends. Their marriage was in jeopardy, and the weight on my shoulders was heavy. God called me to prayer early one morning. Intelligible words soon turned to moanings and groanings as I felt the battle raging; it was obviously a satanic attack. I was feeling their pain, and only the Spirit could pray. In the past we had waged this type of warfare for months, but this time the answer would come quickly.

Later that day, I found out God had sent a woman their way to give them "a word in season." He had spoken clearly through a dream to this dear servant. She immediately obeyed the Lord and relayed the details of it to the struggling couple. The walls melted, and as a result of their obedience to the Lord, their marriage began to heal. Some plant, others water.

The evangelist often reaps where he has not sown. Many times, upon beginning an extended revival meeting, I ask the people attending for the names and addresses of their lost friends and loved ones. The response is always overwhelming. We receive stacks of little notes written on the backs of bulletins, telling of sons and daughters steeped in sin, of prodigals gallivanting around town while Mom and Dad spend sleepless nights in anguish.

Then off we go, our pockets full of directions to homes, our hearts full of anticipation. I've always loved an adventure, and every one of these little notes leads to one. Our visits to these "reported lost" have resulted in everything from cursings to conversions. The Lord has been gracious in giving us much fruit, and many converts are won through our contacts and persistent witnessing. Some reject the message, but most are so shocked to have an evangelist at their door they let us in.

Once inside, we share the love of God, always through a broken spirit and tearful countenance, and we have witnessed miracle after miracle in these times. I always stand amazed as the heavenly Father reaches out, throws His loving arms around the long lost ones, covers their nakedness, feeds them the Bread of Life, lets them sip from the River of Life and restores them. I don't know who weeps more, the newborn believer or the weary warrior!

Then reality sets in: This is not because of me — it isn't the eloquent message or the passionate appeal. Those things played a part, certainly, but the foundation for this conversion had been laid years ago. Perhaps a few yards from the church we'll find the grave of dear Granddad who prayed for years for this prodigal who just came home. Or perhaps an intercessory prayer meeting had been going on for years, pleading for the salvation of this lost soul. In fact, if I were to look back down the spiritual road into years past, I could follow a trail of travailing tears leading to the source of salvation. There she is: Momma, weeping late into the night for her son to come home. Travailing tears.

I am reminded of a Saturday night revival service at Brownsville Assembly of God when a "wave of travail" swept over the congregation. A group of teenagers, many of whom were too weak to stand, were overcome by their burden for souls. As their wails pierced the air, hundreds of sinners raced to the altars. The cry of God's heart had permeated the spirits of these young intercessors. The result of their obedience was marvelous to behold. What a harvest!

To travail means to "put forth strenuous mental or physical exertion." It also refers to the labor of childbirth. Travailing tears flow from the agonizing intercessor over the pitiful, helpless state of the unborn child. The cries of her labor pains pierce the heavens and fall on the ears of God.

Evan Roberts spent ten years of travailing prayer in Wales before the spiritual births of thousands were realized. William Booth agonized in travailing prayer in the secret closet before the countless crowds to whom he ministered experienced new birth. Months of unrelenting cries heavenward finally brought David Brainerd a harvest among the Indians. And George Whitefield's trail of tears led to a trail of souls, both in England and North America.

This all leads to an important question: What is the true worth of a lost soul? In the eyes of the Lord, according to His system of weights and balances, the soul of a man is worth dying for. On the cross and throughout His travail beforehand, Jesus Christ gave spiritual birth to all who believed. He passed through the pangs of birth.

> Who in the days of his flesh, when he had offered up prayers and supplications with strong crying and tears unto him that was able to save him from death, and was heard in that he feared; though he were a Son, yet learned he obedience by the things which he suffered; and being made perfect, he became the author of eternal salvation unto all them that obey him (Heb. 5:7-9, KJV).

We have seen God's value on our souls; it was worth the life of His Son. Now, we ask, how far must we go to see someone come to Christ? Paul went so far as to say, "I could wish that myself were accursed from Christ for my brethren, my kinsmen according to the flesh" (Rom. 9:3, KJV).

I'd like to tell you of an experience that has forever impressed Jeri and me with the value of a soul. We had been in Argentina for several years and were experiencing tremendous results in almost all of our evangelism efforts. But the attack from the enemy was constant. William Bramwell, one of the most powerful preachers of English Methodism during the late eighteenth century, said, "Never look for peace while you proclaim war." We were in constant warfare in the heavenlies. Then, there came an unforgettable physical battle that turned out to be a great spiritual victory.

Jeri awoke one morning screaming at the top of her lungs, "Steve, help me! I can't move!" I asked what was wrong. "It's like someone is jabbing me inside with a knife. Every time I shift, there's excruciating pain. It's like the knife is twisting inside!" She wept uncontrollably from the constant torment. She had had pain for several days, but now it had become totally unbearable.

We immediately called our local doctor, who was quick to provide an explanation: "Those pains are just aftereffects of your recent surgery," he assured her. We had recently lost a child through a tubal pregnancy. The operation had been performed, and the recuperation period seemed to be normal. "Don't worry, Jeri," he told her now. "It will pass. Give yourself a few more weeks."

But where was this pain coming from? Could our doctor be making a mistake? Could he have missed something?

I had never seen my wife in such agony; there obviously was something deeply wrong. Then came the alarm. I placed a call to a German hospital in Buenos Aires, more than five hundred miles away. The German doctor spoke as calmly and professionally as possible, but his words carried the weight of dire emergency: "Get up here immediately," he ordered. "There is something seriously wrong. Your wife's life is in danger."

We caught the next flight out, raced to the hospital and soon found out that the German doctor's suspicions were correct. Jeri was experiencing the pain of another tubal pregnancy, and it was about to explode. She was pregnant with twins!

The reality of the moment drifted over me like a dark cloud. Had we listened to the counsel of our doctor in Southern Argentina, Jeri could have died. After examining her, the German doctor removed five cysts the size of grapefruits, along with the fetuses. The emergency operation was a success. We both knew God had spared Jeri's life, and the agony was gone. But why did she have to go through those months of physical trauma? We were actively involved in serving the Lord. Why such an attack? What was the purpose behind our losing the twins? Was it a test of our loyalty to Christ? What was God's plan in it all?

As a minister, I find it's always easier to give someone else wise counsel than to be the one on the operating table. Within a few short days, however, our answer came.

The German hospital was literally a spiritual battleground. Hundreds upon hundreds of medical professionals raced to and fro helping others while their own spiritual lives were in grave danger. Jeri recognized the depravity of those around her and began sharing the love of Jesus with many. Within a short while, Jeri was giving birth. Her physical birth pangs were about to produce a spiritual babe.

Early one morning the Lord gently revealed part of His plan. Jeri found herself kneeling on the bathroom floor with her nurse, praying! The nurse was weeping tears of repentance; she had given her life to the Lord.

The depth of Jeri's agony, coupled with her confidence in God, was like a word from God to this nurse. In her eyes, Jeri was living the teachings of the Bible. This nurse saw how Jeri had trusted Jesus through every moment, enduring the pain and yet blessing His name — not angry at Him or questioning His omniscience. And now Jeri was able to share with this dear woman how God permitted her to suffer for the sake of a soul. "God loves you so much that He sent me through months of suffering that you might find Christ," she explained. "And Christ loves you so much that He endured the cross, bled and died, that you might find life."

With tears streaming down her cheeks Jeri told the nurse, "You'll never be able to say that God doesn't care about you. Just look how much He cares!" Here she was, kneeling at the foot of the cross in the bathroom of the German hospital.

That is the value of a soul. Yes, God's value system is much different from ours. "For as the heavens are higher than the earth, so are My ways higher than your ways, and My thoughts than your thoughts" (Is. 55:9).

I remember a dear mother who prayed for her son for years upon years. Yet it seemed the more she fasted and prayed, the further from God he went. She agonized in late-night intercession, soaking her pillow with tears. She was feeling the pain of kingdom childbirth. Her son's salvation was not to come easily.

Yet what eventually led to her son's conversion could be likened to the few moments of agonizing pain of a natural birth. At her wits' end, this mother finally prayed, "God, whatever it takes for my son to come to Christ, do it!"

This gutsy statement came just moments before the spiritual birth of her son. She screamed out, passing the pain barrier as an expectant mother would push one last time, and the answer came. Yet she warns mothers and fathers never to utter a prayer like hers unless they mean it.

Her answer came in the form of a serious car accident. Her son was in critical condition, and he was paralyzed from the waist down. The impact of the accident, the fervent prayer of a righteous woman and a river of travailing tears finally had led to his conversion. Now this young man testifies from the confines of a steel wheelchair of how Christ got hold of his life. His testimony rings of the value of a soul.

I believe that for true conversions to take place, for there to be genuine "new birth" experiences, they must develop and happen as fleshly births do. First, there must be the conception, then growth in the womb, and finally the pain and travail of childbirth. Just as a woman must suffer through the delivery of a newborn child, we must feel the pains of spiritual deliveries.

There is no question; we must hurt for the hurting. Yet so many of us spend our lives trying to escape all pain. We want a spiritual epidural to take away all feeling. But pain is part of the process — it's why Christ came. He knew it was important for Him to feel our pain, to experience our misery.

Right now, there is something frightening occurring in the field of clinical medicine that should concern everyone. We have entered the age of mind-altering, personality-enhancing drugs. Forget the play pills of the sixties. Psychopharmacology — the science of drugs that affect the mind — has mapped the mind and now claims to have the power to control it. From antidepressants, taken like M&Ms to alleviate depression, to new drugs intended to control shyness or paranoia, we have launched our society into the false orbit of control. We are dabbling with danger, and our desire to have control will turn into a curse. We want to alter the God-given personality traits that the Lord has used to form history.

Harvard University psychologist Jerome Kagan warns that blunting the edge of human personalities comes with a price tag. "Just as physical pain keeps us from burning our flesh, perhaps mental pain, like that brought on by the death of a child, serves a purpose...one that is defeated by a pill that soothes when one should instead be raging." He further states that some of history's great thinkers and creators were shy. "A society that uses drugs to induce conformity does so at its peril."[3] Shyness is just one of the characteristics under attack. Minor depression, which most often is a God-sent emotion, is also under severe scrutiny.

Let me ask you: Under what circumstances did you come to Christ? In what state of mind? Did you feel bad over the consequences of your sin? Were you suffering inner anguish? Had you hit rock bottom? Were you at the end of your rope?

This is the state of mind most people are in when they come to Christ. Yet science is now implying we don't have to pass through such times. We can pop a pill and fly over all the valleys.

Can you imagine our state if mind-altering drugs had been available throughout the centuries of American history? We could talk for hours about the writers and artists who produced their greatest works during a time of deep emotional trauma. The depth of their heavy moments led to inspiring works that have endured for ages. But what if during their season of suffering they'd gone to the doctor, popped a pill and passed from gloomy to happy? After all, when do the teachings of the Word come alive to you — on the mountaintops or in the valleys?

Now I ask you, when do we pray and travail over a lost soul? It is when we feel the effects of their suffering, when we empathize and enter their misery. "We can never heal the needs we do not feel," Jowett says. "Tearless hearts can never be the heralds of the Passion. We must pity if we would redeem. We must bleed if we would be the ministers of the saving blood."[4]

We must take our compassion to the closet, shut the door and pour out our pain to God. And it's okay to feel bad; the pain and agony one feels over a lost soul is actually a burden sent from God. Furthermore, it's okay to experience stormy emotional weather. Your present state of depression may be God-sent; perhaps the Lord is leading you to a season of travailing prayer. If so, you can be sure He is allowing you to feel the weight of a hurting world.

"Why should I pray that God would take that burden from you?" says Leonard Ravenhill. "He's been trying to put it on you for the last ten years."[5] Having carried such a burden himself for so many lost souls, Ravenhill had acquired keen insight into travail for the lost and the state of the church:

> As the birth of a natural child is predated by months of burden and days of travail, so is the birth of a spiritual child. Jesus prayed for His church, then to bring it to spiritual birth He gave Himself in death. Paul prayed "night and day...exceedingly" for the church; moreover, he travailed for the sinners. It was when Zion travailed that she brought forth...

And further:

> The mother-to-be wearies more as the time of birth draws near, often spending sleepless (but not tearless) nights. Likewise, the lamps of the sanctuary burn the midnight oil as distressed, sin-carrying intercessors pour out their souls for a nation's iniquities. The expectant mother often loses desire for food, and in the interests of the one she will bear, denies herself certain things; and, likewise, denial of food and a consuming love to lie quiet before the Lord seizes believers shamed by the barrenness of the church. As women in pregnancy hide from public gaze (or used to do so), as the time of delivery draws near, so those in travail of

soul shun publicity and seek the face of a holy God.[7]

The American evangelist Charles Finney stated:

> A true believer will labor zealously to bring others to Jesus Christ. They will feel grieved that others do not love God, when they love Him so much. And they will set themselves, often with great emotion, to persuade their neighbors to give Him their hearts. They will be filled with a tender and burning love for souls. They will have a longing desire for the salvation of the whole world. They will be in agony for individuals whom they want to have saved — their friends, relations, enemies. They will not only be urging them to give their lives to God, but they will carry them to God in the arms of faith, and with strong crying and tears beseech God to have mercy on them, and save their souls from endless burnings.

Finney further makes it clear that:

> when the conduct of the wicked drives Christians to prayer and breaks them down, and makes them sorrowful and tender-hearted, so that they can weep day and night, and instead of scolding and reproaching them, they pray earnestly for them. When their actions, both oppositions and apathy drives Christians to their knees in prayer to God, with strong cryings and tears, you may be certain there is going to be a revival.[8]

In his letter to the Galatians, Paul wrote: "My little children, of whom I travail in birth again until Christ be formed in you" (Gal. 4:19). The apostle speaks metaphorically of a second travailing on his part regarding the churches of Galatia; the first was for their deliverance from idolatry and now it was for their deliverance from bondage to Judaism. He seemed to be asking them whether they had ever heard of a mother experiencing second birth pangs for her children.[9]

"Why should it be thought strange that those that are full of the Spirit of Christ should be proportionably, in their love to souls, like to Christ?" writes Jonathan Edwards:

> Christ had so strong a love to them and concern for them as

to be willing to drink the dregs of the cup of God's fury for them. At the same time He offered up His blood for their souls, as their high priest, with strong crying and tears. With extreme agony, the soul of Christ was, as it were, in travail for the souls of the elect.

As such a spirit of love to and concern for souls was the spirit of Christ, so it is the spirit of the church; and therefore, the church, in desiring and seeking that Christ might be brought forth in the world and in the souls of men, is represented, Revelation 12, as "a woman crying, travailing in birth, and pained to be delivered."

The spirit of those that have been in distress for the souls of others, so far as I can discern, seems not to be different from that of the apostle, who travailed for souls, and was ready to wish himself accursed from Christ for others. And that of the psalmist, Psalm 119:53, "Horror hath taken hold upon me, because of the wicked that forsake thy law." And verse 136, "Rivers of waters run down mine eyes, because they keep not thy law." And that of the prophet Jeremiah, Jeremiah 4:19, "My bowels! My bowels! I am pained at my very heart; My heart maketh a noise in me: I cannot hold my peace, because thou has heard, O my soul, the sound of the trumpet, the alarm of war!"

We read of Mordecai, when he saw his people in danger of being destroyed with a temporal destruction, Esther 4:1, that he "rent his clothes, and put on sackcloth and ashes, and went out into the midst of the city, and cried with a loud and bitter cry." And why, then, should persons be thought to be distracted, when they cannot forbear crying out at the consideration of the misery of those that are going to eternal destruction?[10]

When God places a burden on your heart for the lost, don't shrug it off. And don't expect others to understand what you feel. It's personal. Weep for the unsaved. Labor over them. Pour yourself out to God as a living sacrifice for their souls.

In his precious book, *Christ in the Camp,* J. William Jones brings home with great clarity our responsibility to labor over the lost. After spending time in a Civil War hospital, he explains the receptivity of the sick to the gospel. Then he drives home his point by comparing their physical death to their spiritual death:

> In view of all that I have seen, it seems to me, that with the thousands of pale and emaciated forms in the hospitals, with the tens of thousands of sin-sick souls in our camps, a vast responsibility is resting upon the Christians of our state and country. If a surgeon should be filled with remorse to see his patient die for want of attention from himself, how should each Christian, who has not done all he could, feel at each announcement of a soldier's death? And with what pangs of remorse must he behold each mound in the soldiers' graveyard?[11]

Although this was written more than a century ago, it speaks hauntingly to us today. What surgeon would look at a dying patient who could be helped, then callously wipe his hands and leave to attend some sporting event? On the contrary, a dedicated surgeon would agonize through the midnight hour to see his patient brought back to life. How much more should we, as dedicated Christians, agonize throughout the night for the lost and dying?

Charles Finney tells of a woman who had such an unutterable compassion and love for souls, she actually panted for breath almost to suffocation. "What must be the strength of the desire which God feels, when His Spirit produces in Christians such amazing agony, such throes of soul, such travail — God has chosen the best word to express it — it is travail — travail of the soul."

Have you ever wondered who travailed over your soul? Was there someone who perhaps was obscure to the eyes of society but prominent in the eyes of God — someone who travailed over your eminent destruction? As their tears flowed, did perhaps they see more clearly the hope of your salvation? Did they cry out to God as you became more rebellious toward Him?

I'll never forget my mom passing through my room one evening crying out to God. I lay lifeless with some of my friends on the carpet; we were drug addicts and had just injected enough morphine to knock us out for hours. In my numbed state I could barely move, but my mother's cry to God came through loud and clear. I stumbled to my feet and followed her upstairs. As I passed her bedroom I could hear the moanings and groanings of a woman after God for the soul of her son. She travailed. She was giving birth a second time to him. The first time around she brought me into this earthly life — the second time, into eternal life.

Again I quote from the classic, *Why Revival Tarries* (which should be required reading for every Christian):

> Women of the Bible who had been barren brought forth its noblest children: Sarah, barren until ninety years of age, begat Isaac; Rachel's cutting cry, "Give me children or I die!" was answered, and she bore Joseph, who delivered the nation. Manoah's wife bare Samson, another deliverer of the nation.
>
> Hannah, a smitten soul, after sobbing in the sanctuary and vowing vows and continuing in prayer, ignored Eli's scorn, poured out her soul, and received her answer in Samuel, who became the prophet of Israel. The barren and widowed Ruth found mercy and bare Obed, who begat Jesse, the father of David, of whose line came our Saviour. Of Elizabeth, stricken in years, came John the Baptist, of whom Jesus said there was no greater prophet born of women. If shame of childlessness had not subdued these women, what mighty men would have been lost.[12]

I ask you, how much more should we be weeping over our own barrenness? We should be crying out in the night hours, "Give me children or I die!"

But be careful! Childbirth brings responsibility, something few of us want. Are we sure we want to get pregnant? We must be ready to pass through every moment of the process. From the nausea, to the special prenatal care, to the kicking and then the excruciating birth pangs. Once the helpless infant "sees the light," we begin the most difficult task of all — that of raising the child: discipleship. The umbilical cord must be cut, the child cleaned, the crying comforted, the late-night hunger fed and so on. Any parent can continue this list and complete the analogy.

I wrote the following poem during a time of blessed ministry to church leaders and laymen in Florida. The Lord began speaking to me then of the urgency of the hour. On the morning I wrote this, I felt the intensity of the warfare and the necessity to work while it is day. The cost of winning the lost was ringing in my ears. But the Lord said that nothing would come easy.

I saw the battlefield of life littered with victims — some dead, others barely breathing and gasping for help. Blood was everywhere. In the words of the psalmist, I heard the groanings of the prisoners. The enemy was unleashing every weapon, no matter the cost, to win this last battle. "This is not the time of peace," the Lord said. And there is...

No Time to Kill

This is the time to fight for the Lord;
Not the time for ourselves, our treasures to hoard.
This is the time, deep travailing in prayer;
Not the time to lay down His burden of care.

This is the time, crown of thorns I will wear;
Not the time to dream on, of my crown worn up there.
This is the time to be crucified;
Not the time coming soon, stand by His side.

This is the time to run in the race;
Not the time to relax and slow down the pace.
This is the time, His burden to bear;
Not the time for my pleasures or my worldly cares.

This is the time to pick up the cross;
Not the time to drop out and complain of the cost.
This is the time to weep through the night;
Not the time to enjoy the morning so bright.

This is the time to harvest the wheat;
Not the time to sit down and doze off to sleep.
This is the time of suffering and pain;
Not the time to enjoy even more earthly gain.

This is the time to win souls for Him;
Not the time to slide back and wallow in sin.
This is the time of enduring the cold;
Not the warmth of the Son on bright streets of gold.

This is the time to mourn for the dead;

Not the time to rejoice, start dancing instead.
This is the time, the war will not cease;
Not the time we all want, of heavenly peace.

Yes, the timepiece we wear, with accurate detail;
We race to and fro, we must buy and sell.
Our schedule is tight, with precision we dwell;
But His appointment is certain, it's heaven or hell.

To the doctor we run, his schedule to keep;
God's time is more precious, don't drift off to sleep.
Keep pace with the Lord, seek out His will;
His appointments are urgent, there's no time to kill

We should travail with tears over the lost. When you feel the alarm, rush to make God's appointment Don't be late! May God wake us up at midnight, squirming with the pangs of childbirth. And in the still of the night, may He hear a constant dripping — the liquid evidence of our sincere burden for the lost; the agonizing pain of another child passing through the birth canal, from darkness into His everlasting light.

NINE

SWINDLERS AT THE ALTAR

God won't be taken in by false tears.

The gavel slammed down. Stark reality swept across the courtroom as the judge pronounced the sentence. "The state of Alabama finds you guilty on all counts. I sentence you to twenty-five years in the state penitentiary. Next case!"

I was stunned. Along with at least one hundred other spectators, I had just listened to the defendant's incredibly dramatic, heartrending story. For the last twenty minutes he had stood before the judge, his hands and feet cuffed, to plead his case. But the state of Alabama had found him guilty of child neglect and grand theft auto.

My heart had been set adrift by this man's words. Like a master storyteller, he had taken the entire courtroom back to his early childhood, relating in mesmerizing detail the hardships.

> Your Honor, I've had a rough life. My family has always suffered. We've been poor for as long as I can remember. My daddy held odd jobs, sometimes late into the night,

to keep food on the table. I can remember going to bed with such pains in my stomach. There was never enough for everybody. There were six children. I was the oldest. Sacrificing for the youngest was a way of life. The last glass of milk, the last slice of dry bread, always went to little Sarah.

When I was ten, the doctors told my momma I was suffering from an ailment called dyslexia. I couldn't read like my friends. Everything was real confusing for me in school, so I dropped out. I was tired of the other kids laughing at me.

When I turned twelve my daddy died. I had to find work to support the family. We barely made it, Your Honor. Times were hard.

Somehow we survived. Momma got a job ironing clothes, and I delivered groceries. A church down the street helped out with the meals. None of us starved, but it was tough.

By this time half the courtroom was in tears. The defendant himself was sniffling, completely reliving it all. I found myself wiping water from my eyes as well. I thought, *If anyone deserves a pardon, this guy does.*

Yet, behind the bench sat the man who held the defendant's life in his hands. To this day I'll never forget the judge's steely glare. His face seemed so cold, so stern, so unaffected. Why? How could anyone *not* be moved by this very real drama? It wasn't a movie — it was real life. How could the judge just sit there listening, void of emotion?

The defendant continued to unravel his story:

As you know, Your Honor, a man with no education can't get much of a job. By the time I turned twenty I had worked in restaurants, car washes and gas stations. Never had much money. Like everybody else, I drowned my troubles in alcohol and drugs.

I met a girl at the local diner. She was a waitress. We got married and had two kids. Times kept getting harder. We were always cussing and fighting. I've always wanted a better life, but we never had a real chance.

By this time, he had won the courtroom. I'm convinced that a jury would have totally vindicated this poor soul. He closed his story by relating the details of the alleged crime. It went something like this:

> Last Tuesday I was turned down for a good job at the steel factory. I was furious. It was my one chance to make some money and get a better life. My wife was visiting her folks in Tennessee when this took place. I left the two kids at home. I know now that was wrong. Little Aimee is five and my son is only two.
>
> After being turned down, I got drunk. So drunk that I don't remember the next three days. I woke up in the county jail. When they told me the charges, I cried. I didn't mean to neglect my kids. I would never leave them alone for three days. The police say I stole a car. Your Honor, I was stone drunk, out of my mind. I don't remember doing it. Please understand. I'll never do it again.

Tears gushed from his eyes, but he was unable to wipe them because of the handcuffs. Except for an occasional sniffle, the courtroom was deadly silent. Everyone awaited the judge's decision. All were certain he would show mercy.

Turning to the defense lawyer, the judge said, "Does the defense have anything more to add to the case?"

"Nothing, Your Honor. Only to ask that you consider the circumstances and have mercy," the lawyer replied.

It was over in ten seconds. Without remorse — without even a blink of an eye — the judgment came down. Twenty-five years in the state penitentiary.

Shocked beyond belief, I sat fuming in my seat. I had come that day to perhaps help this poor man with his life. We were operating a drug rehabilitation program that often came to the defense of young men such as this. The judge knew of my presence in the courtroom; he was aware of my good intentions to help the man. Why was he so cold, so hard?

In the next few moments, I found myself face to face with the cold, hard facts. In the judge's chamber, I learned that the defendant had been arrested for similar charges on at least seven other occasions. Each time the judge had given clemency. Often, against his better judgment, he had probated the individual hoping for improvement.

Everything had been offered to the defendant, from special training to state handouts. Nothing helped. He didn't want to change. He was a liar and a swindler — what the state called a habitual offender. He had conned me and scores of others in the courtroom, and he had demonstrated no remorse for his crimes. The tears were fake. The story was riddled with exaggerations and lies. And this judge knew the man. Now his words to me were, "Stephen, I do not want to see his face in my courtroom again!"

TEARS OF FEAR

Swindlers at the altar. Who are they? What are they up to? Why does God permit it? All good questions. They deserve good answers.

A swindler is someone who deceives. He defrauds others. He acts selfishly and thoughtlessly. In short, he cheats.

Today, the church of Jesus Christ is full of swindlers. They lie to God. They cheat on their friends. They mock the moving of the Holy Spirit. They're void of true life. They hold to a form of godliness but deny its power in their lives. They wear the cloak of Christianity but shun the cross. They sing God's praises while avoiding His purity. They're swindlers — Judas Iscariots. "What's in it for me?" is their constant question. "What benefit can I obtain from all this religion?"

The prophet Malachi warned:

> "I am not pleased with you," says the Lord of hosts, "nor will I accept an offering from you...You bring what was taken by robbery, and what is lame or sick; so you bring the offering! Should I receive that from your hand?" says the Lord. "But cursed be the swindler who has a male in his flock, and vows it, but sacrifices a blemished animal to the Lord, for I am a great King," says the Lord of hosts, "and My name is feared among the nations" (Mal. 1:10,13-14).

I've seen it again and again: Unrepentant tears flow from the eyes of a swindler caught in the act. With no way out, he cries, cries, cries. Hollywood actors couldn't hold a candle to this display of anguish. But his lies have turned against him. Hemmed in on all sides, he breaks, a pool of tears forming below. "I'm sorry! I'm so sorry! Please forgive me!" he pleads.

In prisons, this is called "jailhouse salvation." A man is in trouble, so he cries out to God. "Get me out of this mess, Lord, and I'll serve You all the days of my life!" Yet he pleads to God with a divided heart. Outwardly it seems so real, but in reality it's just meaningless mumbling.

When will we grasp Solomon's warning? "When you make a vow to God, do not be late in paying it, for He takes no delight in fools. Pay what you vow! It is better that you should not vow than that you should vow and not pay" (Eccl. 5:4-5).

Don't be deceived — God will not be mocked. Swindlers' tears are not tears of remorse but tears of fear. They've been caught — caught in the act. Total exposure is imminent. Their whole way of life is on the line — everything is about to go down the tubes. The old axiom rings true once more: Oh, what a tangled web we weave when first we practice to deceive.

Swindlers at the altar! The bottom line? Nothing is hidden from God. A person can muse for hours about how to cover up, prefabricate every detail and carry it out with the greatest precision, craft a lie with the greatest skill, bury the truth deep in a pit of deception, shovel tons of deceitful dirt into the hole. *There, that should do it!* He brushes his hands clean. He smothers the truth in a blanket of lies. But it's not hidden.

The haunting Word of God warns: "If we had forgotten the name of our God, or extended our hands to a strange god; would not God find this out? For He knows the secrets of the heart" (Ps. 44:20-21).

> O Lord, Thou hast searched me and known me. Thou dost know when I sit down and when I rise up; thou dost understand my thought from afar. Thou dost scrutinize my path and my lying down, and art intimately acquainted with all my ways. Even before there is a word on my tongue, behold, O Lord, thou dost know it all (Ps. 139:1-4).

Caught in the act! But wait, it's only a person you need to fool. "I know what to do," the swindler says. "I'll just role-play. I won't get violent or lash out. I'll just cry. Tears — that's it. Let the rivers flow! Come on, you can do it. Cry like an unrepentant child who's about to get punished. Bawl and squall. It just might work."

"Bingo! What a pushover. I can't believe they fell for it. I deserve an Oscar!"

It's true; any person can be fooled. But God isn't gullible. Another human can be whitewashed, but a swindler cannot con Christ. He can cry buckets of tears. Flood the courtroom floor. Use up a box of tissues and ask for another. But, "Vanity, vanity," cries the preacher in Ecclesiastes!

In a flash, the games will all be over. Have we forgotten our dear brother and sister, Ananias and Sapphira? Why isn't anyone teaching "drop-dead theology"? You know, try to con God and die! One minute you're wheeling and dealing, the next minute you're dead. With your words you give God half, and in exchange He cuts your life in half! The church of today is quick to claim the gifts of God, but why do they negate this portion in the Book of Acts?

Let's read about it:

> But a certain man named Ananias, with his wife Sapphira, sold a piece of property, and kept back some of the price for himself, with his wife's full knowledge, and bringing a portion of it, he laid it at the apostles' feet.
>
> But Peter said, "Ananias, why has Satan filled your heart to lie to the Holy Spirit, and to keep back some of the price of the land? While it remained unsold, did it not remain your own? And after it was sold, was it not under your control? Why is it that you have conceived this deed in your heart? You have not lied to men, but to God" (Acts 5:1-11).

THE EYES OF THE LORD ARE IN EVERY PLACE

Permit me to stop at this point and ask a simple question: Why would someone go to the altar while trying to deceive God in the first place? To be seen by others? Talk about wanting the best of both worlds. It wasn't the money for the land that had been divided; it was the couple's hearts. On the soil of their hearts stood a sign reading, "For Sale, Price Negotiable."

Ananias and Sapphira were swindlers at the altar. They had planned it all together beforehand. "He plans wickedness upon his bed; he sets himself on a path that is not good; he does not despise evil" (Ps. 36:4). In the secret of their home they plotted out the course. Perfect — God wins, we win. Yet what they didn't fully comprehend was the complexity of their crime.

God won't settle for half. Our human understanding protests, "That's not fair. After all, at least they were giving to God. Thousands of others were outside the church squandering everything on themselves. Why did God judge so harshly? Was He establishing His Lordship in the local church? Was He protecting this new group of believers from incoming hypocrites and deceivers? Would the church recover from such a devastating blow?"

I will not enter the territory of these specific questions here; why God did what He did is to many a mystery. Yet one thing remains obvious: Ananias and Sapphira did not weigh the possible repercussions of their deception. What they planned in secret was displayed openly. Any criminal will tell you: Above all, when committing that perfect crime, make sure there are no witnesses. Yet the hard-core truth of the matter is, there will always be three eyewitnesses on the scene: the Father, Son and Holy Spirit.

"Where can I go from Thy Spirit? Or where can I flee from Thy presence? If I ascend to heaven, Thou art there; if I make my bed in Sheol, behold, Thou art there" (Ps. 139:7-8).

"The eyes of the Lord are in every place, watching the evil and the good" (Prov. 15:3).

I want to share with you a deep, personal heartache, something that grieves me more than you'll ever know. It is a pain that has caused me to weep over and over again. All over the world I've had to struggle through this continual throbbing.

I'm speaking of living the half-hearted life. As we continue to lead the lost to Jesus; as the spiritually blind receive their sight for the first time; as the prodigals come home, my constant prayer to God is this:

> Please Lord, help them to associate with sincere Christians. Keep them away from lukewarm youth. May their new-found love for You not be tainted by those who profess to know You but continue to live in darkness. May they meet Christians who pray longer in secret than in public. May they meet warriors, not wimps. As they enter the deacon's home, dear Lord, let them find a worn-out Bible. Place them in the path of purity. Blind their eyes to hypocrisy. Keep them, dear Jesus, from the swindlers. Amen.

We know what happened to our fellow believers, Ananias and Sapphira. They each fell dead in the presence of both God and man. I often wonder what would happen if God permitted them to return to the earth today. You know, one last chance to redeem themselves? What a message they could preach! Centuries ago their mistake spurred a wave of holy fear throughout the land. I believe their message today would do the same.

Think about it; they didn't even have the opportunity to cry. They should have kept part of the land for a burial plot! Little did they realize that their well-executed lie was to become their own execution. Cut down — martyrs to the god of greed. Examples to all. Who was fooling whom?

Why would anyone commit such a crime? Why would someone offer God strange fire? Why would King Saul turn from God and disobey His commands? The filthy litter of swindlers is sprinkled throughout Scripture:

> Then Saul said to Samuel, "I have sinned; I have indeed transgressed the command of the Lord and your words, because I feared the people and listened to their voice. Now therefore, please pardon my sin and return with me, that I may worship the Lord."
>
> But Samuel said to Saul, "I will not return with you; for you have rejected the word of the Lord, and the Lord has rejected you from being king over Israel" (1 Sam. 15:24-26).

Slam! Down goes the gavel. It's over. Thus saith the Lord!

Go ahead — try to cry! Buckle over and belt it out. "Then you returned and wept before the Lord; but the Lord did not listen to your voice, nor give ear to you" (Deut. 1:45).

In truth, the reason such offenses are committed is not because of an overwhelming fear of man but rather because of a lack of a trembling fear of Almighty God. "Transgression speaks to the ungodly within his heart; there is no fear of God before his eyes" (Ps. 36:1). To sum it all up: "Fear God and keep His commandments," says the preacher (Eccl. 12:13).

Now try to replace the terror of standing before an earthly judge with the reality of facing the final judgment, and suddenly things change. Forget the cold stares around the earthly courtroom. Face the One whose stare pierces the darkness. The One whose mere glance strips us naked.

Face the facts — we live constantly under the gaze of three eyewitnesses. "The fear of the Lord is the beginning of knowledge" (Prov. 1:7).

A trial won't be necessary, because the Judge has witnessed every act. We stand defenseless before Him. No fresh evidence will be presented. No one will come storming into the courtroom on your behalf to sway the decision.

God won't be taken in by our tears. He won't be swindled by our heartrending story. We've overstepped the boundaries. Like the man who stood weeping but unrepentant before the judge, it's already over.

Go ahead, cry like a child. Give it your best shot. Lay it on Him.

Slam goes the gavel — guilty as charged!
Slam drop the bodies — Ananias and Sapphira!
Slam sounds the prophet's rejection — King Saul!
Swindlers at the altar — beware! God has not changed!

TEN

TEARS OF REPENTANCE

Deep within every man and woman
there exists a fountain just waiting to erupt —
and it comes when we finally see the reality
of who we are in relation to God.

She couldn't believe her eyes. As her close friends rushed to the altar for forgiveness, she sat simmering. "Lies! It's all a bunch of lies!" Fuming, she stomped out, slamming the auditorium door behind her.

Inside, the presence of the Lord continued melting hearts as though they were of wax. But outside, the fires of hell were raging, hardening Julie's heart toward God's truth. Like a wounded beast, she paced back and forth, ready to lash out. I was her first victim.

"This is a bunch of garbage!" she screamed at me. With words too explicit to repeat, she declared her position. Like a rabid animal about to strike, she vomited out curses. All her inner rage, pain and bitterness became verbal. With fiery eyes she stuck her finger in my face and shouted, "You're spooky, man. Look at what you've done to my friends! Get out of here. I know what I believe, and this ain't it!"

"Then go home," I replied. "Take your beliefs, and go home."

She wouldn't. As if gripped by a force outside herself, she remained.

"Julie, look at me," I ordered. She stopped pacing and stared me down. "You can run, but you cannot hide," I continued.

"Tonight you've been confronted by the cross. You're trapped by truth, and there is no escape. Go ahead, hide. Bury yourself in those bushes. Go home, hide in your basement. Get away from me and my haunting message. But know this — what you feel will follow you. It will never go away. The truth has a way of lingering. It pops up at the most unwelcome moments. You've been gripped by the Spirit, Julie. You can make excuses, but you can't escape."

She looked past me back into the high school auditorium where she saw her friends. The entire gang of teenagers had melted in the presence of the Lord during one of our crusades. I had seen it before — scores of young people openly sobbing in the presence of the Lord.

Julie's friends were weeping uncontrollably. Joy was on their faces, evidence of the peace in their hearts. Rebellion had given way to repentance, and now they were lavishly in love with Jesus. Just a few moments earlier they had been mocking the message. Now they wanted to proclaim it throughout the neighborhood!

It's a mystery. The Bible says, "I, the Lord, search the heart" (Jer. 17:10). Some, upon hearing the precious Word of God, buckle over, melt to the floor and weep tears of repentance. The truth simply pierces them. They allow the examination to take place, and they break over the results.

Still others, however, can hear the same message in the same place, be exposed to the same anointing, yet stiffen up. Like Pharaoh during his days of provocation, they harden their hearts, quench the Spirit and deny His presence.

"And Pharaoh's heart was hardened, and he did not listen to them, as the Lord had said. Then Pharaoh turned and went into his house with no concern even for this" (Ex. 7:22-23). Even when his magicians proclaimed, "This is the finger of God" (Ex. 8:19), he continued in adamant denial. Later, as the plagues worsened, his own servants cried out, "Let the men go, that they may serve the Lord their God. Do you not realize that Egypt is destroyed?" (Ex. 10:7). All to no avail. As if destined for destruction, Pharaoh continued rejecting the obvious.

Today, like Pharaoh, some inwardly scream, "This is a bunch of garbage!" They reason away conviction, smothering their spirit man in a blanket of lies. They curse the cross, spit on the Savior and stomp away, brushing off any possible effect.

"Quit messin' with my life!" Julie shouted.

But then there are sincere tears of repentance. What a welcome sight! They flowed freely from Billy's eyes. A few minutes before, he was hard as a rock. Now soft as clay. Another challenging confrontation with the spirit realm, and Jesus was victor. Watching the teenagers exchange tears on each other's shoulders, I could hear the psalmist: "This is the Lord's doing; it is marvelous in our eyes" (Ps. 118:23).

One of the most striking evidences of an inward work of the Spirit is the presence of sincere, God-invoked tears streaming down the face of a sinner. "Thine arrows stick fast in me, and thy hand presseth me sore. There is no soundness in my flesh because of thine anger; neither is there any rest in my bones because of my sin" (Ps. 38:2-3, KJV). Water gushing from the eyes of a godless heart is often a genuine sign of God's piercing.

Skeptics may discount this; it appears to place surface emotions above a true conviction of sin. I don't deny there are many con artists. (An entire chapter has been devoted to swindlers.) But repentance and tears are a God-ordained marriage — they fit together.

As an evangelist, I cannot lightly overlook someone's tears. I'm well aware of the possibility of deception, but who am I to judge another person's sincerity? Tears soaked my own face at the conclusion of twelve tormenting years of drug addiction. And today I press forward in the hope that a repentant sinner's tears truly are a product of a profound conviction of sin.

The man who led me to the cross never told me, "Wipe your eyes! Get right with God!" No, he detected something genuine in my tears. So he waited and prayed. Yes, the prodigal was coming home. Pain and misery had been bottled up in me for years, and the only form of expression it could take was tears. I went to the cross and cried. I wept for mercy. And the results were permanent.

No amount of books could ever tell the stories of all who have wept sincere tears of repentance. Upon recognizing their sinful state, they turned to Christ, wept out words of sorrow and went on to live a life of godliness.

"Can someone come to Christ and not cry?" you ask. Of course. Yet I believe that deep within every man and woman there exists a fountain just waiting to erupt. It comes from finally seeing the reality of who we are in relation to God and His holiness. Richard Foster, in his book, *Prayer*, notes, "We are not sinners because we commit sinful acts; rather, we commit sinful acts because we are sinners. Through the prayer of tears we give God permission to show us our sinfulness and the sinfulness of the world at the emotional level. Tears are God's way of helping us descend with the mind into the heart and there bow in perpetual adoration and worship."[1]

I've seen it happen too many times to be denied. From stone-faced criminals to star athletes, people melt when confronted by truth.

But the true test of someone's soul is when that person is alone with God. When the door is shut, the friends are gone, the mask is off, that's who we really are. Tears can happen in a crowded room or alone in our home. The Lord simply desires our honesty.

Yet, we are such liars when it comes to our true nature. The Bible says, "Thou dost desire truth in the innermost being" (Ps. 51:6). Can you imagine what our world would be like if everyone gave up role-playing and became real? If we faced up to our true condition and wept openly, the way Jesus wept? We're just a bunch of actors on a stage. But take away our script, wipe away the make-up, toss the costume aside and suddenly we're exposed.

Henry Scougal addressed this subject more than two hundred years ago. In a letter to a friend, he wrote:

> All our wickedness and imperfections, all our follies and our sins, may help to pull down that fond and over-weening conceit which we are apt to entertain of ourselves. That which makes anybody esteem us, is their knowledge or apprehension of some little good, and their ignorance of a great deal of evil that may be in us; were they thoroughly acquainted with us, they would quickly change their opinion.[2]

He continued:

> The thoughts that pass in our heart in the best and most serious day of our life, being exposed unto public view would render us either hateful or ridiculous; and now however we conceal our failings from one another; yet sure we are conscious of them ourselves, and some serious reflections upon them would much qualify and allay the vanity of our spirits.[3]

Henry Scougal penned these words in Scotland at age twenty-six.

For more than two centuries they have called men and women of God to a life of honesty. His words still speak volumes.

Confronted by truth! As the Word of God is preached something happens within the hearer. The one who truly hears the truth finds himself at a critical crossroads: I've been exposed. What do I do?

Godly sorrow leads to godly repentance. King David fell at this intersection. You remember the story: David was at the wrong place, at the wrong time, looking at the wrong woman. "But each one is tempted when he is carried away and enticed by his own lust. Then when lust has conceived, it gives birth to sin; and when sin is accomplished, it brings forth death" (James 1:14-15).

David fell into adultery with Bathsheba and covered up his sin by killing her husband, Uriah. But he was plagued by pain; the weight of guilt was too much to bear. Then the prophet Nathan came on the scene. Looking past the king's crown, he saw a coward and a criminal. His words pierced David's heart: "You are the man!" the prophet proclaimed.

Oh, how I thank God for bold men and women of God! For those who live under the fear of God and not the fear of man! You might kill your Uriah, but the deadly truth remains. Once again you are trapped by truth. Your cover-up failed. Now you're naked, exposed to the elements. You did it! No one knows the truth about it except God. But that's enough. It's over. Now every deceptive detail is delivered with haunting accuracy. The crime so perfectly planned and committed. What waste! What foolishness!

Uriah's corpse rotted while his innocent blood screamed heavenward. But the stench was not of flesh and blood. It reeked from David's heart — "the rottenness of your heart!" God cries. "It's the foul odor of your uncleanliness!" Guilty! Guilty as charged!

David repented. He was a weeper, and the sacrifice he brought to the altar was a broken spirit. "A broken and a contrite heart, O God, thou wilt not despise" (Ps. 51:17).

David went from the depths of sin to the heights of forgiveness. He knew what it was like to live outside of fellowship with God. He knew the agony of defeat, the inexpressible joy of forgiveness.

His story is repeated countless times around the world each day. A preacher preaches, and someone with a need listens. The Word of God pierces deeply.

The Word of God is living and active and sharper than any two-edged sword, and piercing as far as the division of soul and spirit, of both joints and marrow, and able to judge the thoughts and intentions of the heart. And there is no creature hidden from His sight, but all things are open and laid bare to the eyes of Him with whom we have to do (Heb. 4:12-13).

The preacher places a standard before the listener: a sinless example; a perfected man; One who was in all ways tempted yet was without sin; One who loved not His life even while facing death; One whose purpose was that no one should perish but that everyone should come to repentance; One who suffered more abuse and ridicule in a few hours than most men do in a lifetime; One who did it all for someone else.

When this truth hits home, when the Holy Spirit begins to convince a wayward person of his dilemma, when all heaven comes down and all hell looks up to see it — oh, what ecstasy and joy! The battle rages on the bloody soil of the heart, and all the vain arguments burn up like chaff at the Word of the Lord!

For centuries men and women of God have witnessed godly sorrow take place coupled with tears of repentance. Jonathan Edwards in his book on the life of David Brainerd, a missionary to the American Indians in the eighteenth century, wrote:

> Sundry persons, who before had been slightly awakened, were now deeply wounded with a sense of their sin and misery.
>
> "One man in particular," Brainerd wrote, "had been made to feel the sharpness of God's two-edged sword. He seemed to be pierced at the heart with distress; all the wickedness of his past life was brought to his remembrance afresh; and he saw every vile action replayed as if he'd done them yesterday."
>
> A number of older men also were in distress for their souls — they couldn't keep from weeping and crying aloud. "Their bitter groans were the most convincing, as well as affecting evidences, of the reality and depth of their inward anguish."[4]

Remember Julie, Billy and the gang? At first they all mocked the message, pretending to be oblivious to the Spirit. They flippantly joked, cut-up and laughed among themselves. Then it happened. As I preached Christ and Him crucified — as He was lifted up — all heaven came down. Dry eyes became moist. Billy fought the tears. Hoping to hide, he discreetly brushed away the Spirit's touch but to no avail God had won. Truth had conquered. The sinner's prayer followed, soaked in sincere tears of repentance. A new name written in glory!

But what about Julie? She was Billy's girlfriend. As I mentioned previously, some grow hard as others melt. Some curse while others cry. As the Spirit of the Lord came down in that particular crusade, everyone was suddenly exposed.

Like Adam and Eve, caught in the act, Julie fled from His presence But there truly is nowhere to hide. God requires a response — yes or no, accept or reject, in or out, love or hate, heaven or hell. She stood at the crossroads.

Julie clawed herself away from the hold of conviction. She wrestled and won that night. But in the end she'll lose. The round may be over, but the match is yet to be determined.

Go ahead — use every trick in the book. Kick and bite. Pull out your brass knuckles. Swing at Him. It's all in vain — just batting the wind.

Run out of the building. Scream at the preacher. Slander the Savior. Julie held me at bay, at arm's length. "No closer!" she screamed. "Stay away from me!"

You can keep the preacher at arm's length but not the Lord. "Behold, the Lord's hand is not so short that it cannot save; neither is His ear so dull that it cannot hear" (Is. 59:1).

One day it will all be over. No more kicking and screaming — just weeping and gnashing. No more hell-fire-and-brimstone preachers — just eternal punishment. Pain and anguish will find no relief. Slap away the cup of water here on earth — then crave just a drop of it in hell.

A word to the preacher: Thank the Lord upon witnessing true tears of repentance. Rejoice in the honesty. Thank God someone said yes.

A word to the backslidden and sinner: Dig deep. Search your heart. Be honest with yourself and God. Don't lie. May you experience a tearful revelation.

I close this chapter with a quote from Henry Ward Beecher: "No man can go down into the dungeon of his experience and hold the torch of God's Word to all its dark chambers, and hidden cavities and slimy recesses, and not come up with a shudder and a chill, and an earnest cry to God for divine mercy and cleansing."[5]

Weep it out, my friend. Let the filth and corruption rise to the top and drift away on a stream of tears.

ELEVEN

TEARS IN A BOTTLE

Does God really understand
our pain or sorrow when we cry?
Can He sincerely empathize with our feelings?

It was two o'clock in the morning. Esther heard noises outside the house and nudged her husband to investigate.

A few minutes later he returned, grabbing his .32 caliber pistol from the dresser drawer. "It's only a raccoon, Honey," he assured her. "It's probably after the chickens. I'm going to have to kill it. Be right back."

Esther and Ralph enjoyed life to its fullest. They had moved from Michigan to the Seattle area right after their wedding and had settled into a lovely, country home on Vashon Island.

Esther especially harbored a deep love for animals and music. To help her through the ordeal of the shooting, she decided to retreat to the soothing sound of her organ. While Ralph went after the raccoon, Esther sat down to play, hoping to muffle the shots when they rang out. Her decision would prove fatal.

As Ralph swung open the front door to go outside, the little animal scurried under the automobile. Ralph fired two shots, both missing the intended target. Then the raccoon leaped to the roof of the car, drawing what would be the fatal shot.

It was called it a freak accident, never to happen again in a million years. The bullet from Ralph's pistol passed through the wall of the house, ricocheted and struck Esther in the chest as she was seated at the organ. She fell to the ground, wounded. A few days later she was pronounced dead at the Seattle hospital.

It was one of those tragic "if only" situations. If only they had slept through the disturbing rustling of the raccoon. If only the raccoon had run away after the first bullet cracked the midnight air. If only Esther had stayed in bed while Ralph went after the little animal. If only the organ had been placed a few inches to the left or right. If only the first bullet had hit the target. If only they had decided not to buy a handgun and had bought a shotgun instead. The list goes on and on and ends only in futility.

We all know that bad things happen to good people. There is no one to blame. We can wonder for the remainder of our days why such a thing would happen as it did with Esther, and we'd never come up with the answer. The bottom line is what happened, happened, and now it was time to accept it.

I was three years old when this devastating incident took place. Esther was my mother's older sister. I remember the scene that took place afterward as if it were yesterday.

I was playing with my toys in the living room when the phone rang. It was Uncle Ralph calling from Seattle. Mom answered, and within moments, she was weeping beyond control. I dropped my toys and went to the kitchen table where she sat.

As Mom was told of the freak accident, she couldn't believe her ears. "But she was so young — so full of life — so loving," she uttered. I could hear her voice cracking from the deep emotional trauma. "Why Esther?" she sobbed. Her sister was dead. Mom knew she would be unable to attend the funeral because she was pregnant with my younger sister, Susie. The realization of not ever seeing her sister again only added pain to her misery.

This heartbreaking event took place over three decades ago. At the time, I was unable to fully understand the situation. But I did realize one thing: My mom was hurting, and I wanted to help. Yet how do you comfort someone who is mourning over such a sudden death? I decided simply to draw close to her and to be there if she needed me.

What I remember the most were her tears. A steady stream fell to the table. Little did I know that, figuratively speaking, I was collecting her tears as a living memorial to the tragic death of her sister Esther. As my mother wept, I lifted up an imaginary bottle, filled it with tears and stored it forever in my memory. Now as an adult I can reach back through time, scan the shelves of my mind and pull down the little bottle entitled "Mommy's Tears Over the Death of Her Sister Esther." Tears in a bottle.

Most of us have experienced similar situations throughout our lives. If we could just stop the treadmill of everyday life and remain still for a few moments, our minds would take us back to tearful experiences we've never forgotten.

Not long ago a good friend, Christine, related an incident she had stored in her memory. The story was not tragic, but it had remained memorable due to the presence of tears.

> My dad is an adult Sunday school teacher at our church. He approached me a few days ago and asked if I would relate a particularly memorable situation that took place during my childhood concerning parenthood. No matter if it was good or bad, he wanted to hear an honest experience of my views as a child under his parental authority. The event came to me immediately.
>
> "Dad, the most shocking event of my childhood is something that you probably won't even remember," I told him. "I was a teenager and, in direct disobedience, had sneaked out of the house while you and Mom were eating out. Upon finding out, you displayed an emotion that we kids had never witnessed."
>
> I guess he was expecting me to share about a severe punishment or perhaps a fabulous family vacation on the beach. Or perhaps the Christmas morning when I saw under the tree a glimmering new bicycle. Or maybe all the time he spent side by side with me, haggling over math equations. But I was right — he didn't remember anything about this little ordeal.
>
> "Dad, you called a family meeting. The courtroom was the kitchen, you were the judge and jury, and I was the defendant. I remember as you entered the room you had a

look of remorse. Rather than wrath, I saw sorrow. Sitting down at the table you began to relate your shortcomings to the family. You said that you were a failure as a father, and you took the blame for my actions. Your expressions displayed such sadness and dismay. And then it happened. You began to cry."

"I had never seen you cry, Dad," I continued. "I had seen anger, laughter and a wealth of other emotions, but I had never seen you weep. Your tears were my punishment. I was guilty. No more evidence needed to be presented. It was worse than a spanking, far more severe than grounding. You were weeping over my disobedience. It had a profound effect on my behavior for years to come. As you wept, the tears were a constant dripping. It was like the Chinese water torture we've all heard about, when the enemy has to endure days of steady drips of water on his forehead. Your tears did more for me than years of parental counseling. That was the day, Dad, that I saw your heart. Your tears made me want to change."

On that day, unknowingly, Christine had done the same thing I'd done when my mom heard of the tragic death of her sister Esther. She had bottled up her dad's tears as a living memorial to the death of her disobedient acts. Now years later she was reading the label of that little bottle: "Daddy's Tears Over My Disobedience."

Most of us could share similar stories of unforgettable events engraved in our minds through the presence of tears. Like a gentle river, the flow of tears has a way of cutting through the hard ground and leaving an eternal imprint on our minds. Many of us can follow the tracks of our tears back to the source. Unconsciously, we set up an "historical marker" sign. Yes, we're all tear collectors.

The apostle Paul referred to the power of tears in his second letter to Timothy: "I thank God, whom I serve with a clear conscience the way my forefathers did, as I constantly remember you in my prayers night and day, longing to see you, even as I recall your tears, so that I may be filled with joy" (2 Tim. 1:3-4). Timothy's tears left a deep impression on the mind of Paul. The apostle stored up those tears and referred back to them in this most precious letter.

The idea of collecting tears as a memorial has been going on for centuries. In fact, some civilizations have actually carried out what we have done mentally, collecting tears in little bottles as memorials to those who have died.

These little bottles, called lachrymatories, are still found in great numbers in ancient tombs. The custom was to collect the tears of the mourners and preserve them in bottles. These bottles were made of thin glass (or, more generally, of simple pottery, often not even baked or glazed) with a slender body, a broad bottom and a funnel-shaped top. If the friends of the deceased were expected to contribute their share of tears for these bottles, they often hired cunning women to cause their eyelids to gush out water.

This ritual of collecting insincere tears was very offensive to sensible people. The Latin historian Cornelius Tacitus (A.D. 55–120) revealed the disdain many had for this custom: "At my funeral let no tokens of sorrow be seen, no pompous mockery of woe. Crown me with chaplets, strew flowers on my grave and let my friends erect no vain memorial to tell where my remains are lodged."

Collecting tears not only was common among the Romans, but was in practice at an earlier period among the Eastern nations. In some of the mournful Persian assemblies, a priest would go to each person at the height of his grief with a piece of cotton in his hand, with which he carefully collected the falling tears. He then squeezed the tears into a bottle, preserving them with the greatest caution.[1] This somewhat illustrates Psalm 56:8: "Thou hast taken account of my wanderings; put my tears in Thy bottle; are they not in Thy book?"

In her book, *The Fountain and the Furnace,* Maggie Ross writes, "It is possible that the woman who bathed Jesus' feet with her tears (Luke 7:38), was pouring out her bottle of tears. The Greek verb could be translated in this way. Having found her Lord, she no longer needed to hold to herself all her joys and sorrows, but could pour them out and be free. Her tears became undammed to flow with the waters of life into the river of life."[2]

There was another similar practice during the times of the psalmist. When a person was ill or in great distress, his friends went to see him, taking along a tear bottle. As the tears rolled down the sufferer's cheeks, they were caught in these bottles, sealed up, and preserved as a memorial to the event.

It is important to note here: In order for these tears to be collected, there had to be a visitation. I can imagine David crying out to the

Lord, "Visit me, and behold my tears. Oh, visit me with Thy salvation for without such a visit there will be no bottling of my tears. Behold my anguish. Keep them before Thee by way of remembrance, and when Thou seest the bottle, O think of him whose tears it contains." In Psalm 42:3, David writes, "My tears have been my food day and night."

Does God really understand our pain or sorrow when we cry? Can He sincerely empathize with our suffering?

In reading the book of Genesis, I came across the wonderful verse, "Let Us make man in Our image, according to Our likeness" (Gen. 1:26). It's fairly clear that this passage of Scripture is saying that God made us like Himself. "Here is the text," writes Joseph Parker. "Here is the distinct assurance that God created man in his own image and likeness; in the image of God created He him. This is enough to ruin any Bible. This is enough to dethrone God. Within narrow limits any man would be justified in saying, 'If man is made in the image of God, I will not worship a God who bears such an image.'"[3]

We all see Reverend Joseph Parker's point. But remember, we are now dealing with fallen man. Before the fall, the beauty of God's human creation radiated with His characteristics. The likeness of God consisted in the immortality of the soul and in His holiness and innocence. Man was endued with powers and faculties and was capable of knowing, loving and fearing God. And to top it all off, he was given power and dominion over the lower creation, just as God had power over the spirit world.[4] Yes, the love, the caring, the fellowship with God, the wisdom, all were part of man's makeup before the fall.

Today we must look to the man Christ Jesus in order to fully understand this text. As we follow Him and walk in obedience to His Word, the goodness of God begins to surface. We find buried beneath tons of carnality a treasure just waiting to be discovered. His likeness runs deep, like rivers of crude oil bubbling beneath the surface. As we pursue the Lord, we burrow through layers of hard ground, pleading for His treasure to come forth. "I want You!" we cry. "I want to be just like You, Lord Jesus! I want to be rich in You, Jesus." We dig deeper and deeper, and then it happens: We strike oil! The love of Christ comes bursting forth from our innermost being. We drench ourselves and those around us. We are soaked in His presence.

If you will look to Him, you will see fruit in your life that bears the image and likeness of God. Be like Him, and you will be in His image.

Yet here is my overarching point: Just as we sense sorrow and have our "nights of weeping," so does God. He grieves just as we do.

He first created us, and then He went the final mile for us by clothing Himself in fleshly garments, to experience everything we go through. Never forget this powerful passage of Scripture concerning the life of our Lord: "In the days of His flesh, He offered up both prayers and supplications with loud crying and tears to the One able to save Him from death, and He was heard because of His piety" (Heb. 5:7). No one has filled up tear bottles as our Lord Jesus has.

Are you passing through a personal Gethsemane? Are you alone? Are your friends standing by your side or are they asleep in the distance? Are you at that place with God saying, "Not mine, but Thy will be done"? Is it hard to drink of the cup before you?

Jesus has been there. He is holding the bottle, catching every teardrop.

Are you teary-eyed from running the race? We've all experienced tears welling up as we went running against the wind. Its brisk force, cutting across our eyes, dried out the moisture. Our body reacts by crying, soothing the dryness. Are the winds of adversity blowing across as you run this race? Jesus has been there. He is holding the bottle, catching every teardrop.

Are you experiencing rejection? Have your friends and family forsaken you? Are you clinging to God's promise, "When my father and my mother forsake me, then the Lord will take me up" (Ps. 27:10, KJV)? Remember, Jesus has been there. He is holding the bottle, catching every teardrop.

Are you tired of your wanderings? Do you feel like a hunted fugitive, like David, with the pressure clamping down on all sides? Do you find yourself going from one dark cave to another or from wilderness to wilderness? Do you have no place to lay your head? Jesus has been there. He is holding the bottle, catching every teardrop.

Is the world crashing down all around you? Are you standing on a hill, beholding the agony of this life, as Jesus beheld the city of Jerusalem? Are you seeing what could have been a perfect situation, but sin has separated you from God's best? Are you feeling the effects of rebellion? Do you feel the darkness of destruction? Jesus has been there. He is holding the bottle, catching every teardrop.

I ask you, "Have you discovered the precious well of tears deep down inside?" It has been said that in the Far East water is so scarce that if a man owns a well he is rich. Battles have been fought for the possession of a well.

But every man does own a well — a deep well of tears. A tear is agony in solution. And by divine power it may be crystallized into spiritual wealth and all burdens lifted.[5]

If you're in a severe spiritual drought, craving a drop of moisture, perhaps today a deep well is there to be discovered. Not without, but rather within — there you'll find your spiritual oasis. Let the tears well up and flow freely. God is patiently waiting to collect every drop.

Perhaps you can relate to what I'm saying. You may need refreshment from the Lord as never before. Like David of old, you are crying out, "Oh Lord, you see my wanderings." My friend, He is with you. "Weeping may endure for a night, but joy cometh in the morning" (Ps. 30:5, KJV).

Read the following verses as His promise to you during this dark crisis: "Arise, shine; for your light has come, and the glory of the Lord has risen upon you" (Is. 60:1). "For waters will break forth in the wilderness and streams in the Arabah [desert]. And the scorched land will become a pool, and the thirsty ground springs of water" (Is. 35:6-7).

Let God bottle the tears. One day you'll look back, peruse the shelves, and marvel at this precious time of your life in the Lord.

Jesus has experienced every tear of joy and every tear of sorrow. "For we do not have a high priest who cannot sympathize with our weaknesses, but one who has been tempted in all things as we are, yet without sin. Let us therefore draw near with confidence to the throne of grace, that we may receive mercy and may find grace to help in time of need" (Heb. 4:15-16). Our High Priest strolls through the corridors of our homes, having filled bottles of His own tears, then leans over and gently places an empty bottle under our eyes. "Weep, my beloved — I'll catch every drop," He assures us. "I will remember your suffering. I am recording your pain."

The great London preacher Edward Irving, who endured incredible hardships, said it so beautifully:

> Oh, the eternal value of godly tears. They are good tears which burst from our hearts when we look upon Him whom we have pierced, and weep as a mother that weepeth for an only son. The tears which Christ wept over Jerusalem, fallen and impenitent, foreseeing its relentless doom. The tears of compassion which he wept over the sorrows of the house of Lazarus. The tears which Paul shed, when, in the

city of Ephesus, he went, by night and by day, from house to house, entreating the people to be reconciled unto God.

Not the bitter and disappointed mood of Jonah when he was exceedingly displeased and very angry because the Lord had relented of His threatenings against Nineveh, and entreated God, saying, "Take, I beseech thee, my life away from me, for it is better for me to die than to live" (Jon. 4:3); but the mood of Jeremiah the prophet, when he exclaimed, "Is there no balm in Gilead? Is there no physician there? Why, then, is not the health of the daughter of my people recovered?"...Oh that my head were water, and mine eyes a fountain of tears, that I might weep day and night for the daughters of my people!" (Jer. 8:22; 9:1, KJV).

Not the tears of pride which come reluctant from the hardened heart, like water dropping from the flinty rock, but the tears of pride humbled and convinced by the power of God. These tears flow copiously like the stream which issued from the rock when it had been smitten by the wand of Moses, the messenger of God.

Not the tears of natural desire after a worldly good, nor the tears of natural sorrow for a worldly good removed, but the tears of spiritual desire after spiritual good. Or perhaps the tears of sorrow when God hath hidden His countenance or removed our candlestick out of its former place.[6]

God is very interested in our sorrow, and He records more than we could possibly imagine. He is a serious collector. To store His findings He uses books, bags and bottles.

In His books He stores our names and our deeds: "I ask you also to help these women who have shared my struggle in the cause of the gospel, together with Clement also, and the rest of my fellow workers, whose names are in the book of life" (Phil. 4:3). "And I saw the dead, the great and the small, standing before the throne, and books were opened; and another book was opened, which is the book of life; and the dead were judged from the things which were written in the books, according to their deeds" (Rev. 20:12).

In His bags are our sins. "My transgression is sealed up in a bag, and Thou dost wrap up my iniquity" (Job 14:17). What a precious truth! Once our transgressions are sealed in His bag, they are nailed to the cross (Col. 2:13-14) and then cast into the sea (Mic. 7:19).

And in His bottles we find our tears. "Put my tears in Thy bottle" (Ps. 56:8). Understandably the bags and the bottles are just metaphors, but they serve as tremendous tools to help us understand the wonderful ways of the Lord.

It's interesting to note that no mention is made of the quality of the bottle. I'm certain that if reference had been made, such as, "Put my tears in Thy precious bottles," the pious, religious leaders of old would have made a doctrine of it. They would immediately have become more concerned over the size, quality and material of their particular tear bottle.

There would be, without a doubt, a snazzily dressed television evangelist sending you a pewter tear bottle with your initials for every fifty-dollar donation; a silver tear bottle with your name engraved for every one hundred dollars; a gold-plated bottle etched with intricate, angelic beings surrounding your name for every five hundred-dollar donation; and of course, for the more generous givers of ten thousand dollars or more, a platinum tear bottle, inlaid with diamonds, with your name spelled out in precious jewels!

While we're on the subject of bottles, I'd like to talk about bottle collecting. Collecting old bottles, to some, is as serious as watching the stock market is to others. Many bottles carry a face value of thousands of dollars. For example, if you have a last-century, seven-inch, rectangular, pinkish-colored bottle with the words Jacob's Cabin Tonic Bitters on it, I suggest you take it down to your local car lot and cash it in for a new ride, or call the creditors and let them know the check is in the mail. Your bottle is worth close to ten thousand dollars![7] Sobering, huh? A serious collector is always on the lookout for a rare treasure.

Most old bottles have imperfections, such as dents in the glass, crooked necks, bubbles and so forth. They are valuable for every imperfection and highly desired by collectors.[8] Terms such as applied lip, kick-up bottom, blob seals, whittle marks and sheared up are unknown terms to the novice. But to the avid bottle connoisseur you're speaking the common language.

Now God is a serious collector, but His interest is not in the value of the container but rather the purity of the content. Man always judges by the outward appearance, but God goes by the inward.

Of all things for God to collect, you ask, why would He store up tears? Could it be to show how precious they are in His sight and to suggest that they are preserved for a future use? The tears that His children shed and give to Him to keep cannot be tears of rebellious or insincere weeping. True godly tears will be given back one day to those who shed them, converted into refreshment by the same power which of old turned water into wine.

> Think not thou canst weep a tear,
> And thy Maker is not near.[9]

As kids, we used to sing an old tavern song, "A Hundred Bottles of Beer on the Wall." Let's change a couple of letters and use it to look afresh at God's incredible collection of tears:

> A hundred bottles of tears on the wall,
> A hundred bottles of tears.
> Take one down, pass it around,
> Ninety-nine bottles of tears on the wall.
>
> Ninety-nine bottles of tears on the wall,
> Ninety-nine bottles of tears.
> Take one down, pass it around,
> Ninety-eight bottles of tears on the wall.

We could easily start in the millions as our eyes scan the inconceivable collection of bottles lining the walls of God's tear chamber. Rows and rows of earthen vessels, large and small, holding the precious remains of the saints. William S. Plumer (1802–1880) once said, "The road to heaven is soaked with the tears and blood of the saints."

I don't know how God would categorize His tear collection. Would they be in alphabetical order? Could you find the tears of Abraham, say, on the far left, then browse through millions of bottles until you came to those of the great Moravian missionary Nicholas Zinzendorf on the right? Or would they be categorized alphabetically under subject titles such as those we will discuss in the remainder of this chapter?

TEAR BOTTLES OF HUMAN SUFFERING AND HARDSHIPS

Let's reach up to a shelf and randomly pull down a bottle. Look closely at the label. Perhaps we're about to behold the liquid remains of a bloodied martyr. Or perhaps this bottle holds the anguish of the family left behind.

Here's one that looks interesting. The name on the bottle is Isabel Brown, wife of John Brown of Priesthill, martyred April 1685. Why would her tears be eternally remembered in this storehouse of suffering?

Let's read a portion of her ordeal:

It was a time of intense persecution in Scotland. At the king's command a whirlwind of activity had led to the death of scores of Christians throughout the land. Anyone who would not bow to the king was considered a heretic and sentenced to death.

John Brown fell victim to a man named Claverhouse, sent forth by the king to carry out these cold-blooded murders. It was said of Claverhouse that he actually thirsted after the blood of the reformers. He and his men, having heard of John Brown's loyalty to the Lord Jesus, headed into the fields to find this follower of God.

They arrived early one April morning. John Brown's confession was all the evidence they needed, and they got it. The verdict was out: The sentence was death.

"Go to your prayers, for you shall immediately die," Claverhouse ordered. His tone was so harsh as to even fill his own troops with amazement. On Brown's family it had a different effect. His wife — who was great with child, held another in her arms, and had six-year-old Janet at her side — stood while her husband prayed "that every covenanted blessing might be poured upon her and her children, born and unborn, as one refreshed by the influences of the Holy Spirit, when He comes down like rain upon the mown grass, as showers upon the earth."

When Claverhouse could bear Brown's prayers no longer, he succeeded (after interrupting him twice with the most blasphemous language), in raising him from his knees. John said to his wife: "Isabel, this is the day I told you of before we were married." He added, with his usual kindness, "You see me summoned to appear in a few minutes before the court of heaven, as a witness in our Redeemer's cause, against the ruler of Scotland. Are you willing that I should part from you?"

"Heartily willing," she answered, in a voice that spoke both her regard for her husband and her submission to the Lord, "even when God called her to bow before His terrible trials."

Once again John Brown began to pray. This ignited a fury within Claverhouse. He immediately ordered six of his soldiers to shoot Brown, but Brown's prayers and conduct had disarmed them from performing such a savage action. They stood motionless. Fearing for their mutiny, Claverhouse snatched a pistol from his own belt and shot John Brown through the head.

Claverhouse's troops slunk from the awful scene. Then their commander, like a beast of prey that tramples and howls over a fallen victim, insulted the tender-hearted wife while she gathered up her husband's shattered head. He taunted her with jeers: "What think ye of thy husband now, woman?"

"I have always thought good of him," she said, "and now more than ever!"

"I should kill you, too!" he shouted. She replied, "I doubt that your cruelty could go that length; but how will ye answer for this morning's work?"

With a countenance that belied his words, he answered, "To men I can be answerable, and as for God I will take Him in my own hands." Thus saying, he hastily put spurs to his horse and left her with the corpse.

Isabel tied up John's head with her napkin, composed his body, covered it with her plaid, and when she had nothing further to do or contend with, sat down on the ground, drew her children to her, and wept over her mangled husband. She was pregnant and widowed with Janet and little Isabel. Their teardrops fell, but not to the ground. God was there, catching every last drop.[10]

Such are tear bottles of human suffering and hardships. We could spend ages reading the names of those who have truly suffered. I think of the countless numbers of little children who have suffered the trauma of war in this century alone. Oceans of tears have been collected as an eternal memorial to their pain.

Before leaving God's tear-bottle collection, let's spend just a few moments scanning the shelves under another interesting category.

TEAR BOTTLES OF REPENTANT SINNERS

Abraham Wright penned these beautiful words more than three hundred years ago:

> While we remain in this veil of misery, God keeps all our tears in a bottle; so precious is the water that is distilled from penitent eyes: and because he will be sure not to fail, he notes how many drops there be in His register. It was a precious ointment wherewith the woman in the Pharisee's house (it is thought Mary Magdalene) anointed the feet of Christ; but her tears, wherewith she washed them, were more worth than her spikenard.[11]

The nineteenth-century British pastor Charles H. Spurgeon, who was well-known as the prince of preachers, wrote, "I don't know when I am more perfectly happy than when I am weeping for sin at the foot of the cross."

The Word of God is rich in stories of repentance — some sincere, others insincere. Suddenly a name comes to mind. How about Esau. Surely God saw the tears of Esau? Yet, our eyes grow weary looking through all the *E*s on the bottles. There is no Esau! "Weren't his tears sincere?" we ask. Didn't God record his remorse over selling his birthright to his brother Jacob? Doesn't Genesis say that "he cried out with an exceedingly great and bitter cry" to his father, Isaac? "Bless me, even me also, O my father!" (Gen. 27:34, KJV). What about Esau's tear bottle?

Look again at the Word of God:

> See to it that no one comes short of the grace of God; that no root of bitterness springing up causes trouble, and by it many be defiled; that there be no immoral or godless person like Esau, who sold his own birthright for a single meal. For you know that even afterwards, when he desired

to inherit the blessing, he was rejected, for he found no place for repentance, though he sought for it with tears (Heb. 12:15-17).

The tears fell but not in God's bottle. Is it possible today to "trade our birthright" for the pleasures of sin? Like a single meal, sin is pleasurable for a season. But later, is it possible to weep buckets of tears and still find "no place" for repentance?

Now, scanning the shelves, we come across a very familiar name. It is the name of a great warrior for the cause of Christ. Take a close look at the label: Simon Barjona, better known as Peter.

This is the man of whom Jesus said:

> Blessed art thou, Simon Barjona: for flesh and blood hath not revealed it unto thee, but my Father which is in heaven. And I say also unto thee, that thou art Peter, and upon this rock I will build my church; and the gates of hell shall not prevail against it. And I will give unto thee the keys of the kingdom of heaven: and whatsoever thou shalt bind on earth shall be bound ın heaven: and whatsoever thou shalt loose on earth shall be loosed in heaven (Matt. 16:17-19, KJV).

But Peter had a tough road ahead of him. You see, there was a day coming when his words, "Thou art the Christ," (Matt. 16:16, KJV), would come back to haunt him.

We're astonished at the size of his bottle. As we lift it from the shelf we find it full to the brim with tears. When did Peter weep enough to fill such a large vessel?

As we search the Scriptures, we find the answer. We find Peter later at a crisis point in his life. He had spent more than three years with his Master. With his own eyes he had witnessed miracle after miracle. Now at the trial of Jesus we find the apostle warming himself around the fires of the ungodly. The wrong place at the wrong time around the wrong fire! Why didn't he remember the words of the psalmist? "Blessed is the man that walketh not in the counsel of the ungodly, nor standeth in the way of sinners, nor sitteth in the seat of the scornful" (Ps. 1:1, KJV).

The Word of God records this event in haunting detail. "And a little later the bystanders came up and said to Peter, 'Surely you too are one of them; for the way you talk gives you away.' Then he began to curse and swear, 'I do not know the man!' And immediately a cock crowed" (Matt. 26:73-74). "And the Lord turned, and looked upon Peter. And Peter remembered the word of the Lord, how he had said unto him, Before the cock crow, thou shalt deny me thrice. And Peter went out, and wept bitterly" (Luke 22:61-62, KJV).

How could the same man who had just uttered these words, "Thou art the Christ, the Son of the living God," just a short time later, with the keys of the kingdom of heaven dangling from his hands, curse and say, "I tell you I don't know Him?"

I think we all understand Peter's dilemma. Very few believers throughout the span of Christian history have not denied the Lord at one time or another, either in our words or in actions. We have shrunk under the pressure and given in to the clamor of the crowd.

But bless the name of Jesus; His mercies are new every morning! There is forgiveness! We find hope even in Peter's life as Scripture unfolds it. He was forgiven and used greatly in the Master's service.

Krummacher, in his treatise, *The Suffering Saviour,* touches on this traumatic scene:

> Peter, by the look of his Master, is wholly dissolved in grief and humiliation. He covers his head with his mantle, as if he were unworthy to appear before God or man and begins to "weep bitterly." These are the tears of which it is written, "Put them into thy bottle; are they not in thy book?" and from the sowing of which a harvest of joy is promised. Like the pearly drops which burst in spring from the branches of the vine, they testify of the existence of life; and in the eye of the sinner, announce to Satan the loss of his suit and the end of his triumph. O how much is reflected in these tears![12]

True tears of repentance. You won't find Esau's, but you will find Peter's. True, tearful repentance is bottled up for eternity.

We glance over and see another category of tears upon the shelves of God's tear chamber.

INTERCESSORY TEARS OVER THE LOST

Why such few bottles?
Another category sits nearby.

Here we see millions upon millions of tiny containers. A sea of sorrow from innocent eyes.

The list of categories goes on and on. A million bottles of tears on the wall. God's tear collection. Every drop speaks volumes.

The lachrymatories that are unearthed today from ancient tombs are filled with dust. The tears evaporated centuries ago. But God's bottles and their contents are preserved for eternity — always within arm's reach of the Lord. He treasures His collection. Every droplet is as sweet incense; every bottle a reminder of the sincerity of His children.

Perhaps on judgment day they'll be used as evidence for or against us.

Now back to His tear chamber for one last selection. You scan the labels. But you can't seem to...

"What's that you say?" the attendant inquires.

"I can't find my bottle."

"Oh, come on. Surely there must be a mistake. Look again. Your name is there somewhere, isn't it?"

TWELVE

WEEPING IN THE FIELDS

*A great cloud of witnesses
and a great legacy of tears
urges us on from heaven.*

S it down in this chair, and draw it up to that table," the old man said to the visitor. "Now put your elbows down upon the surface and rest your head upon your hands. Let your tears fall. That's the way my pastor used to do."

The old parishioner was speaking of the beloved minister Robert Murray McCheyne, who had just gone to be with the Lord at age twenty-nine. Young McCheyne had lived his life with tears in his eyes and a sheaf of wheat on his shoulders. He had wept in the fields, and he had rejoiced at the reward of the harvest. He openly confessed with the patriarch Job: "Have I not wept for the one whose life is hard? Was not my soul grieved for the needy?" (Job 30:25).[1]

In the Psalms we find a text that will bring results to all our labors. This passage is the key to unfolding the mysteries of spiritual harvest: "He who continually goes forth weeping, bearing seed for sowing, shall doubtless come again with rejoicing, bringing his sheaves with him" (Ps. 126:6, NKJV).

The evidence rings loud and clear: Wept-out sermons produce a bountiful harvest. Just as earthly showers soften dry ground, so tears soften hearers' hearts. And as we toss seeds of truth on the freshly moistened soil, a remarkable occurrence takes place: New life begins to spring forth!

I have seen this truth borne out time after time in open-air campaigns and in one-on-one evangelism. I'm not talking about out-of-control emotionalism, but rather a person's innermost being crying out for a touch from the living God.

During a street meeting in Spain I saw a teenage girl from Finland come to Jesus, weeping uncontrollably as she prayed. Then two more teenagers came forward, wiping tears from their eyes. They asked me if people always cry when we talk to them about God.

"The reason you're crying," I explained, "is because of the deep need in your hearts to know your Creator. You've been searching for happiness in everything except Jesus. But God loves you so much that He sent me halfway around the world to invite you to come home to Him. I know the Lord, and He sent me to talk to you. He is here with us right now — we're in the presence of the Lord. Don't turn away."

They prayed and received Christ. The list goes on and on of people's remarkable confrontations with the Lord during a sweet shower of tears.

The psalmist speaks of the overwhelming joy that follows such an encounter. Here we have a song that speaks not only of abiding in the Lord but of being fruitful in Him:

> When the Lord turned again the captivity of Zion, we were like them that dream. Then was our mouth filled with laughter, and our tongue with singing: then said they among the heathen, The Lord hath done great things for them. The Lord hath done great things for us; whereof we are glad.
>
> Turn again our captivity, O Lord, as the streams in the south. They that sow in tears shall reap in joy. He that goeth forth and weepeth, bearing precious seed, shall doubtless come again with rejoicing, bringing his sheaves with him (Ps. 126:1-6, KJV).

I ask you, what could be more thrilling than to have the proof of a fruitful harvest bundled up on your back?

The natural and spiritual parallels of sowing and reaping are profound yet elementary. Whenever the children of God were in trouble, they remembered their times of deliverance. A little thought, a bit of meditation, a brief moment of musing on the Lord's mighty hand and they quickly changed their tune. "This is my infirmity: but I will remember the years of the right hand of the Most High. I will remember the works of the Lord: surely I will remember thy wonders of old. I will meditate also of all thy work, and talk of thy doings" (Ps. 77:10-12, KJV).

As we labor for the Lord in the present, it is very important to remember the wonders of the Lord in the past. Practically speaking, as we begin to sow for this year's harvest, we must remember God's past provision. We must activate our memories and muse over His miracle-working power. "Look at what He's done," says the psalmist. "He's brought me up out of the miry pit!"

Most of us can testify of such great deliverances, yet how quickly we forget His miracles of the past! Like a smoke screen, time hazes over our memory, and bogged down once more in the pit of despair, we wonder where He's gone. But if you remember the victories of the past, a flood of spiritual strength will prepare you for your present battle.

Consider Charles Finney, the nineteenth century American revivalist. As he interceded over sinners, he saw in the natural some very difficult, rocky soil. Yet in the spirit he saw an incredible harvest. He began his intercession by musing over past victories, reminding God, "Now concerning the salvation of these people, O Lord, You know that I'm not accustomed to being denied." What a gutsy statement of faith! Finney's remembrances of God's faithfulness transported him to a heavenly state of trust. "Do it again, dear God! Bring us another plentiful harvest!"

For the past two decades I have used my remembering-back mode in scores of crusades. As I stand before crowds, I look toward heaven, close my eyes and remember the wonders of the Lord. I meditate on the miracles of those "impossible people" who have melted in the arms of the Lord.

As my mind wanders down the spiritual roads of my past, I see sprinkled along both sides spiritual road markers, signposts proclaiming all the ways God has met me during difficult times. There was the time He brought me through an incredibly impossible financial situation. The time He saved a member of my family from self-destruction; the time He healed my body from a serious sickness. As I meditate along the roadside, soon a new faith begins to build within me. Strength arising from sheer joy gives me courage to face the present battle. The people before me sense my faith in God, listen to His wonders of old and are drawn to believe in Him.

The Lord almost always uses people when He performs His deliverances in our lives. But we must never forget who does the delivering. As ministers of the gospel, we must remember where our message of deliverance comes from. The bottom line is that the Lord "did loose the loins of kings; to open doors before him so that gates will not be shut: I will go before you and make the rough places smooth; I will shatter the doors of bronze, cut through their iron bars" (Is. 45:1-2).

Nevertheless, we need to take a look at what I call "the weeping sower." You may ask, "Why would a sower or farmer weep? Shouldn't sowing be a time of great expectation? Why would he weep over the seeds?" The answer comes as we study the life of those who have carved their living from the hard, rocky soil of the earth.

The farmer in ancient Palestine frequently had to sow his seeds with an armed man attending him to prevent him from being robbed of his seed. Tristram, in his book, *Land of Israel,* says:

> In descending the hill from Bethany we saw an illustration of the wretched insecurity of the country, in a drove of donkeys laden with firewood for Jerusalem. Each donkey was attended by a man armed to the teeth with pistols, swords, and a long gun; and in one little valley — the only one beyond Bethany where there was any cultivation — each ploughman was holding his firearm in one hand while he guided the plough with the other.[2]

In his book, *The Land and the Book,* Thomson relates that in seasons of great scarcity, poor peasants parted sorrowfully with every measure of precious seed they cast into the ground. It was like taking bread out of the mouths of their children, and in such times many bitter tears were actually shed over it. The distress was frequently so great that the government often was obliged to furnish seed, or none would be sown.[3]

Matthew Henry takes the sowing analogy one step further: "There are tears which are themselves the seed that we must sow; tears of sorrow for sin, our own and others; tears of sympathy with the afflicted church; and tears of tenderness in prayer and under the word."

Indeed, the work of evangelism is hard, dusty labor. My friend Carlos Anacondia, a powerful Argentine evangelist, says there is no satisfaction that equals busting rocks in the fields and getting dirty. His definition of evangelism consists of nitty-gritty, hard work in the field of battle because he knows that so much depends on the state of the unbeliever.

As a sower of the precious seed, I first take a good look at the soil. I walk around and across the heartland, inspecting it, and the Lord is always faithful to reveal its character. Later, as I preach, the reactions on faces often reveal the condition of the heart. I've trod on land that is both rocky and worn. Some heartland has had too much growing on it for too long. But within a few moments of tearful preaching, much of that soil begins to moisten. Heaven-sent nutrients begin to fall, giving new hope to the barren land.

Often the Word of God comes like an earthquake, shaking the spiritual soil of listening hearts. A little shaking begins to uncover the rocks and stones, and now the work of removal begins. I might remove a stumbling block of doubt by sharing stories of miraculous healings. A boulder of disbelief melts in the Lord's presence. Now comes the time of working the soil, the sin-baked crust of the heart must be turned. My tears fall, moistening the desert land. Soon the gospel plow moves in. Furrows are dug, and the valuable seed is dropped in.

My weeping continues. Delivering the Word of God often overwhelms me. Like the farmers of old who wept over their precious seeds, I often feel a tremendous loss. Will there be fruit? Am I casting my pearls before swine? God promised, "My Word will not return void." Will I see the harvest, or will one who comes after me benefit from all this work? Dear God, all I ask is that Your fruit remain.

The seeds of the sower are now placed into the hands of the Savior. Unless a grain of the wheat falls to the ground and dies, it cannot bear fruit.

Helen Spurrell, in her wonderful translation of the Old Testament, beautifully illustrates verse six of Psalm 126: "He that goeth forth persistently with weeping, Bearing the seed-basket; Shall undoubtedly return with singing, Bearing along his sheaves."[4]

George Horne, in his commentary on the Psalms, takes us through the process:

In the sweat of his brow the husbandman tills his land, and casts the seed into the ground, where for a time it lies dead and buried. A dark and dreary winter follows, and all seems to be lost; but at the return of spring universal nature revives the soil. The once desolate fields are covered with corn which, when matured by the sun's heat, the cheerful reapers cut down, and it is brought home with triumphant shouts of joy. Here, O disciples of Jesus, behold an emblem of thy present labor and thy future reward! You "sow," perhaps, in "tears." You carry out your duty amidst persecution and affliction, sickness, pain and sorrow. You labor in the church, and no account is made of your labors, no profit seems likely to arise from them. Then you must drop yourself into the dust of death, let all the storms of that winter pass over you, until your form has perished and you see corruption. Yet the day is coming when you shall "reap in joy," and plentiful shall be your harvest.

For thus thy blessed Master "went forth weeping," a man of sorrows and acquainted with grief, "bearing precious seed" and sowing it around him, till at length his own body was buried like a grain of wheat in the furrow of the grave. But He arose, and is now in heaven, from when he shall "doubtless come again with rejoicing," with the voice of the archangel and the trump of God, "bringing his sheaves with him." Then shall every man receive the fruit of his works and have praise of God.[5]

I feel the toil of the harvest every time I step into a park to preach. The work began in the closet; now on any street corner or plaza the war is raging and the battle is white-hot. The sins of the world beat down like the hot sun at midday. The winds of adversity blow across the field. We are battling the elements of man's carnal nature; the world, the flesh and the devil are poised to kill the first signs of new life. "We wrestle not against flesh and blood, but against principalities, against powers, against the rulers of the darkness of this world, against spiritual wickedness in high places" (Eph. 6:12, KJV).

As some hearers slump deeper into despondency, a familiar passage from Genesis comes to mind: "And the Lord said, My spirit shall not always strive with man" (Gen. 6:3, KJV). I wonder, though: *How long can we expect the Lord to continue? What more does He have to do? A little more wooing? A little more gentleness?*

Yet, the voice of God comes to me in such moments and says, "Be careful, Steve. Those who seem so adamant against Me are actually the closest."

My mind goes back to the hard soil of my own heart. My heart was solid as bedrock; the topsoil was destroyed. It reminds me of the book of Joel: "The field is wasted, the land mourneth; for the corn is wasted: the new wine is dried up, the oil languisheth...The beasts of the field cry also unto thee: for the rivers of waters are dried up, and the fire hath devoured the pastures of the wilderness" (Joel 1:10,20, KJV).

My life had been destroyed by the ravages of sinful locusts. Then like an angel of the Lord, a broken man filled with the Spirit of God came into my life. He was not there to condemn me but to show compassion. Within minutes of meeting him I was kneeling at the cross. Then came the blessed promise spoken through Joel: "I will restore to you the years that the locusts have eaten" (Joel 2:25, KJV).

Not only was He saving me, but now He was going to heal my heartland. My life would be soaked in a heavenly downpour. Fruit would begin to grow; life would sprout from my once barren, rock-hard soil. As I remember my dilemma, a new surge of the Savior's love pours forth from my heart for the hardened sinner. Maybe there's hope; there had been for me. Tears flow.

Years earlier I had learned that the word *compassion* means to "suffer together." Someone has said that empathy is your pain in my heart. We may not know their names, but we can feel their pain. And the plowing and sowing continue. Tears soak the people's hardened hearts as they listen to someone who cares. What might have seemed like strong words to some bring healing to the bones of others. We see the restoration begin as they move toward the Savior.

"If you are a Christian, then you too, will have bowels of mercy," (Col. 3:12, KJV) writes Philip Doddridge.

> The mercies of God, and those of the blessed Redeemer, will work on your heart, to mould it to sentiments of compassion and generosity. You will feel the wants and sorrows of others. You will desire to relieve their necessities; and as you have an opportunity, you will do good both to their bodies and their souls; expressing your kind affections in

suitable actions, which may both evidence their sincerity and render them effectual.[6]

There must also be boldness and fervency on our part. Weeping in the fields is for men and women of God not for spiritual jellyfish. God does not cater to cowards. "For whoever is ashamed of Me and My words in this adulterous and sinful generation, the Son of Man will also be ashamed of him when He comes in the glory of His Father with the holy angels" (Mark 8:38).

When I think of boldness, I am reminded of the thousands of cult missionaries around the world. We meet them on the streets in every nation. The sad truth is that most of us are dumbfounded at the rapid growth of cults within our society. "I don't understand it," we say. "How could anyone be so blind as to follow someone like that? Don't they see the erroneous doctrine? They sold everything to follow this man, who is obviously a false prophet. How can they be so naive as to be led away like a sheep to the slaughter?"

Could it be that many are joining up because compassion has been shown? In his study on religions entitled *The People's Religion: American Faith in the Nineties,* George Gallup, Jr., gives two reasons why people are attracted to cults. These should act as a wake-up call to the church of Jesus Christ:

1. The need for leadership and a father figure
2. Unhappy lives and a feeling of hopelessness[7]

Still others cited the need for a deeper meaning to life, as well as the failure of churches to answer spiritual needs.[8]

It should come as no surprise to us that the two main reasons people join cults have nothing to do with the doctrine and everything to do with the desire for fellowship and care. That is all the more reason for Christians to take on the compassion of the Lord. People are willing to follow someone who cares. Lost humanity is ready to give in to someone who truly gives out. The old saying is true: "People don't care how much you know until they know how much you care."

Also, as we weep in the fields we must learn to look past facades. We must remember that the topsoil of people's lives may be covering layers of sin-hardened ground. Some may stand before the hammer of the Lord radiating with self-sufficiency, but inside they're suffocating.

It's not difficult to discern traces of thirst in the faces of those whom we meet in the common way. If we take our stand at the corner of the street and scan the faces of the passing crowd, only now and then do we gaze upon a countenance that has peace. How rarely do we see joy, serenity, a healthy satisfaction. "We are confronted by an abounding unrest! The majority of people seem to be afflicted with the pain of unsatisfied want. The very faces are suggestive of a disquieting thirst."[9]

G. D. Watson (a great holiness preacher born in Virginia in 1845) offers us the following depth of understanding:

> No sinner can be made to weep by a mere, cold, formal sight of his sins. Mount Sinai made the Jews tremble, but it did not make them weep. And so the denunciation of sin, or the portrayal of it, can never of itself produce penitential tears. It is only when the sins are seen under the soft, melting Light of infinite pity and love, that the heart is broken and the tears flow. Law may reveal sin, but nothing in the universe except love will make a man hate his sins. Water may be locked up in ice, but you cannot drink it till it is melted, and it takes the warmth of the tenderest love to bring forth the waters of repentance.

His few words on the subject speak volumes of truth.

I have seen many young people, upon sensing the blessed forgiveness of the Lord, immediately launch into the harvest field. A shower of tears from the preacher had drenched their sin-parched hearts. Having experienced such a downpour, they immediately enlist to work in the fields. With no more than a Bible in their hands and Jesus in their hearts, they move to the front lines, ready to take on the enemy with unquenchable zeal.

I will never forget a young man named Milton who was saved during our Colombian crusade. God had miraculously delivered him from alcohol and drugs, and his experience with the Lord was genuine. He wept tears of repentance, then out poured tears of joy. Within one hour of his conversion, he said to me, "Can I work with you on the streets?" What a question! And what a pleasure it was to work with such a fresh, enthusiastic recruit. I can testify to the wisdom of D. L. Moody, who said: "As soon as a young man is saved I put him to work. I work him day and night. I believe that for one man killed by overwork in the cause of Christ, ten thousand die from laziness." Side by side, new converts learn the importance of weeping in the fields for the lost.

I received the following letter after preaching at a Bible school in Buenos Aires. The letter was the result of a wept-out message on the compassion of the Lord:

> Today made an incredible impact in the lives of the students. Every one of us fell to our knees weeping before the Lord. After chapel we went to our scheduled classes. My classmates continued to weep. We could not control our tears. The professor had to stop teaching. The burden was too much to bear. Broken and tender, we began to pray. Another student had just testified of the fire of God falling on her during the preaching. She was shaking uncontrollably and spoke of a renewed call of God on her life. Another, sobbing, was convicted of wasting precious time while the world was racing towards eternal damnation.

These results would never have taken place if the message had not been soaked in tears. During the great Irish revival of 1859 S. J. Moore wrote:

> I have frequently observed that immediately on securing, as they feel safety in the Savior for themselves, and in their deep and glowing gratitude have ascribed to Him all the glory of their deliverance, they begin with overflowing compassion and intense urgency to plead with Jesus for poor sinners, that they too may come and enjoy salvation, and glorify Christ. More than once I have been necessitated to cause young persons to be carried out of public meetings to prevent utter confusion. From silent prayer on their knees in the pews they would rise, and standing on the seats, the tears profusely flowing from their eyes, with all the anxiety of a life and death struggle, they would call upon sinners to come to Jesus, and upon God's Holy Spirit to bring them to Jesus. This compassion for sinners, or for the glory of Christ in their salvation, cannot be controlled. While the impulse remains you must yield to it, however timid and unobtrusive.[10]

We must come to the point in our labors that if we do not see others come to the Lord, we are grieved. We should grieve and mourn over their spiritual blindness and death. As a farmer would weep over an unfruitful harvest, we should likewise shed tears over empty silos.

> It is written about John Bunyan that he carried this weight upon his shoulders. He knew the worth of an interest in Christ, by his own experiences of the goodness of God, showing him, on the one hand, his natural pollution, guilt and enmity, and the wrath that was due to him thereby; and the virtue of the blood of Christ on the other, to free from all. And from that experimental knowledge did flow hearty desires, and fervent prayers, that the work of God might be effectually wrought on sinners, especially those among whom he labored in the word and doctrine; and matter of grief was it to him, when he did not see conversion.[11]
>
> Of John Welch it is told that he would spend long hours on his knees by his bedside, even on winter nights, praying and weeping in the darkness, with only his plaid flung about his shoulders to shield him from the cold, and that his wife, poor creature, would expostulate with him and bid him return to his rest, only to receive the reply: 'Oh, woman, I have the souls of three thousand to answer for, and I know not how it is with many of them."[12]

The burden of souls was constantly resting upon Welch's shoulders. Here was a spiritual farmer who sowed in tears and reaped in joy.

I ask you, Do you witness as a dying person to dying people? Do you carry the weight of the world upon your back? Can you feel others' suffering? Do you hear the cries of the future damned?

One of England's greatest evangelists carried the burden of the Lord to America. George Whitefield's compassion often moved him to tears:

> As he opened up the treasures of God's infinite mercy and the riches of redeeming love to their view, he wept to think how long they had been unknown or despised by many, and with what base ingratitude thousands would probably still turn away from them. As one who saw their immortal being in jeopardy, and their souls standing on the verge of

irretrievable ruin, he hastened, with joy in his countenance and tenderness in his heart, to tell them of One who was "mighty to save," and that "now was the accepted time, and now the day of salvation."

He carried the weight of the Great Commission and knew the worth of never-dying souls. The evil of sin, the danger of impenitence, the powers of the world to come, the glories of heaven and the unutterable miseries of the regions of hell were visibly present to his own mind; and of these, "out of the abundance of his heart" he spoke to others. He could not be calm, he could not be apathetic on such themes as these. With much of the melting tenderness of Him who wept over Jerusalem, he spoke of these things to all that resorted to him. His vivid eye beamed with the glow of tenderness, and his tears, as he spoke, oft-times moistened his little Bible or bedewed the ground. The place in which he stood was a Bochim — a place of weeping.[13]

Like Whitefield, Welch and Bunyan we must make compassionate contact with our eyes. People must not only hear our sermons but see it dripping down our faces. It was said of D. L. Moody that he never referred to hell without tears in his voice. He understood the language of tears. Our cries in the secret closet of prayer must transport us on a river of tears to the cries of the lost.

In order to weep in the fields we must first move to the field. Yet, sadly, most of us never make it past the front gate. Watchman Nee, author of *The Normal Christian Life,* once wrote, "In a world system darkened with the smoke of the pit, how we rejoice to meet saints who are fresh with the clean air of heaven."[14] While I couldn't agree more with him, I am also deeply troubled. You see, to fully understand his statement, we must consider the source.

Watchman Nee was a persecuted, God-fearing, soul-winning saint of the Lord. His heart was deeply rooted in the realities of servanthood. He carried upon his shoulders the burden of the Lord. And he saw everything through the eyes of eternity. Thus, suffering for righteousness' sake was, to him, merely temporal; only what was done for Christ held value.

In this way, he understood personally the verbal persecution laid upon our Lord, as described in Luke 15:1-2. The religious leaders clamored and complained about Jesus' lifestyle, constantly spitting accusations against Him. "This man receives sinners and eats with them" (v. 2). they protested. And indeed, Jesus was guilty as charged.

This is the bottom line of Mr. Nee's statement: The fresh air of heaven can be enjoyed only after having intimate contact with the stench of this world. He would be appalled at modern Christians' over-indulgence of food, fun and fellowship and our hypocritical attitudes toward the ungodly.

You see, Jesus lived in the smoking section. His garments were constantly darkened by the smoke of the pit, while His heart remained clean with the fresh air of heaven. Likewise, Watchman Nee spent abundant time with sinners; he too lived in the smoking section. And he knew how refreshing it is to have a clean shower from heaven after a long, hard day of toil in the dusty harvest fields on earth. He knew the satisfaction of savoring the meat of the Word after laboring for the Lord all afternoon in the hot sun. He knew the sweet taste of living water from the eternal fountain after sweating behind the gospel plow. And he appreciated the light of the world much more after working in the dark of the night.

Are you consumed with the plight of man? Do you dine with deceivers? Can you converse with the condemned? Are you a friend of sinners? Do they know it? Do they feel it? Do you often smell like their smoke?

"We ought to weep because we have no tears for the lost," proclaims Leonard Ravenhill. "We ought to blush that we're unashamed. We ought to get down before God and repent that we've no broken heart. A wet-eyed preacher can never preach a dry-eyed sermon."

Maybe you remember the last time you sat with your family in a restaurant, enjoying a meal, when a group of rowdy, foul-mouthed young people slipped into the next booth. As they proceeded to rant and rave in unrighteousness, literally cursing God, every emotion in you — from fear to outrage — crept up from within.

Their smoke filled the room, contaminating your privacy; not the smoke of tobacco but the haze of hell. Their cloud hovered over your table and made everyone uneasy. Ungodliness, filth and the stench of the pit turned your mini-vacation into an encounter with hell. As they danced with the devil and dined with demons, you shoveled in the last morsel from your plate, called for the check, paid the bill and hurried for the door. Out you went but to where?

There is no escape from sinners. We share this planet with the ungodly. And we have to remember that many of us were just the same as these people (and perhaps that wasn't so long ago). How can we have grown so righteous, so untouchable?

What if people with the good news had fled our presence after smelling our breath? What if they had slammed the door in our face after hearing our foul mouth? What if they had said, "Hopeless heathen, blind fool, God-hater. One day you'll pay. Come on, let's get out of here!"

Could it be that sinners smell the stench of our pious spirituality? Could it be they would turn their back on anyone who offered them Jesus because of what we've presented to them with our lives and attitudes?

Jonathan Edwards was appalled at the hypocrisy of many Christian workers:

> Some make a great show of love to God and Christ, but they have not a love and benevolence towards men, but are disposed to contention, envy and revenge. Many will suffer an old grudge to rest in their bosoms for years, living in bitterness of spirit towards their neighbor. On the other hand, there are others, that appear as if they had a great deal of benevolence to men, but have no love to God.[15]

Robert Murray McCheyne responded to pious attitudes by exhorting:

> Deal gently and tenderly with your unconverted friends. Remember...you were once as blind as they.[16]

Susan Huntington, the dear friend of John Wesley, George Whitefield and Philip Doddridge, said there are three elements of the renewed soul:

1. A complete hatred of sin
2. A devout love to the Redeemer
3. Love and goodwill to man

"Am I really a child of God?" she questions during a time of self-examination.

> Do I honestly and heartily desire to be free from the cor-

ruption which underlies my nature, and which makes me an alien from my Father's house? Does my heart go out in tenderness and love to Him who hath borne my iniquities and by whose stripes I am healed? And with this love in my soul, is it my heart's desire and prayer to God to bear my part, humble though it be, to bring others to this Savior of lost men? For this is the fruit of faith.[17]

I challenge you to ask yourself these questions:

- Does God want me as a weeping worker in His fields?
- Am I willing to pay the price for the harvest?
- Will I give up my "most precious seeds" and patiently wait for winter to pass?
- Will I labor as unto the Lord of the harvest?

Here, once again, is our text — the key to unlocking the mysteries of spiritual harvest: "He that goeth forth and weepeth, bearing precious seed, shall doubtless come again with rejoicing, bringing his sheaves with him" (Ps. 126:6, KJV).

"Speak every time, my dear brother, as if it were your last," said George Whitefield. "Weep out, if possible, every argument, and compel them to cry, 'Behold, how He loves us.'"

I'd like to reemphasize a thought from Richard Baxter mentioned in a previous chapter: "Go to poor sinners with tears in your eyes, that they may see you believe them to be miserable, and that you unfeignedly pity their case. Let them perceive it is the desire of your heart to do them good."

The great cloud of witnesses wail to us from heaven: "Weep over your flock!" cries the message from the heart of McCheyne. "Weep for the world!" we learn from Whitefield. "Weep for your neighbor!" pleads the passionate call of Baxter.

"Weep in the fields!" says the Lord of the harvest. Amen!

NOTES

Chapter One
A Personal Famine

1. C. H. Spurgeon, *Treasury of David*, vol. 3 (Grand Rapids, Mich.: Baker Book House, 1983), 53.
2. Andrew Bonar, *Memoirs and Remains of the Reverend Robert Murray McCheyne* (Edinburgh: Oliphant, Anderson & Ferrier, 1881).
3. Ibid.
4. John Flavel, *A Treatise on Keeping the Heart* (New York: The American Tract Society, 1835), 85.
5. J. B. Stoney, *Ministry*, vol. 1 (Lancing, Sussex: Kingston Bible Trust, 1985), 14.
6. Herman Venema (1700s), quoted by C. H. Spurgeon, *Treasury of David* (London: Passmore and Alabaster, 1878), 74.
7. Edna Dean Proctor and A. Moore, *Life Thoughts, Gathered from the Extemporaneous Discourses of Henry Ward Beecher* (New York: Ford, Howard & Hulbert, n.d.), 20.
8. *Letters of George Whitefield* (n.d.; reprint, Edinburgh: Banner of Truth Trust, 1978).

Chapter Three
The Sorrow of the Lord

1. Thomas à Kempis, *The Imitation of Christ,* trans. William C. Creasy (Macon, Ga.: Mercer University Press, 1989), 23.
2. Francis Parkman, *An Offering of Sympathy to the Afflicted* (London: James Monroe and Company, 1842), 133.
3. Ibid.
4. John McClintock and James Strong, *Encyclopedia of Biblical, Theological, and Ecclesiastical Literature,* vol. 3 (New York: Harper Brothers, 1894), 1008.
5. Ibid.
6. Phineas Fletcher, untitled poem from *Hail, Gladdening Light, Music of the English Church, The Cambridge Singers* (Great Britain: Collegium Records, 1991), 113.
7. C. H. Spurgeon, *Treasury of David,* vol. 2 (n.d.; reprint, Grand Rapids, Mich.: Baker Book House, 1983), 462.
8. D. A. Harsha, "Savior's Agony by Joseph Hall," *Devotional Thoughts of Eminent Divines* (American Tract Society, 1866), 61.

9. Richard J. Foster, *Prayer: Finding the Heart's True Home* (San Francisco, Calif.: Harper, 1992), 44.

10. Stephen Charnock, *The Existence and Attributes of God,* vol. 1 (Grand Rapids, Mich.: Baker Book House Co., 1979), 96-397.

11. Spurgeon, *Treasury of David,* vol. 2.

12. Thomas, I.D.E., *The Golden Treasury of Puritan Quotations* (Edinburgh: Banner of Truth Trust, 1977), 41.

13. Charnock, *The Existence and Attributes of God,* 397.

14. C. H. Spurgeon, *Treasury of David,* vol. 1 (n.d.; reprint, Grand Rapids, Mich.: Baker Book House, 1983), 188.

15. Bonar, *Memoirs and Remains of the Reverend Robert Murray McCheyne,* 153.

16. C. H. Spurgeon, *Treasury of David,* vol. 1, 83.

17. Horatius Bonar, *The Night of Weeping or Words for the Suffering Family of God* (Robert Carter & Brothers, 1856), 151-153.

Chapter Four
Big Boys Don't Cry

1. William H. Frey II and Muriel Langseth, *Crying, The Mystery of Tears* (Minneapolis, Minn.: Winston Press, Inc., 1985), 4.

2. Ibid.

3. Stuart Cosgrove, "Men Who Cry," *Statesmen and Society* 3 (November 1990): 32.

4. *Essence* 21 (November 1990): 38.

5. "Cry! It's Human," *Glamour Magazine,* August 1991, 212.

6. William J. Hart, *Hymn Stories of the Twentieth Century* (Boston, Mass.: W. A. Wilde Co., 1948), 98-99.

7. From the song, "Onward Christian Soldiers," text by Sabine Baring-Gould.

8. From the song, "Battle Hymn of the Republic," text by Julia Ward Howe.

9. F. W. Boreham, *A Temple of Topaz* (Philadelphia, Pa.: Judson Press, 1928; reprint, New York: Abingdon Press, 1951), 30-31.

10. Frey and Langseth, *Crying, The Mystery of Tears,* 99.

11. *Memoirs of Reverend Charles G. Finney* (New York: A. S. Barnes & Co., 1876), 19.

12. Rob Warner, *Prepare for Revival* (Great Britain: Hodder & Stoughton, 1995), 84-85.

13. Frey and Langseth, *Crying, The Mystery of Tears,* 96.

14. Roberta Israeloff, "Are You a Crybaby? Here's Why, Baby!" *Cosmopolitan* 214 (April 1993): 123.

15. Thomas Scott, *The Force of Truth* (Edinburgh: Banner of Truth Trust, 1841), 93.

16. Frey and Langseth, *Crying, The Mystery of Tears,* 102.

17. Richard Foster, *Prayer: Finding the Heart's True Home* (San Francisco, Calif.: Harper Collins Publishers, 1992), 45.

Chapter Five
Dry-Eye Syndrome

1. See note 1 in chapter 4 for publication information.

2. Charles B. Clayman, M.D., *The American Medical Association Encyclopedia of Medicine* (New York: Random House, 1989), 966.

3. Ibid.

4. S. Norman Sherry, M.D., "How to Calm a Crying Baby," *Ladies Home Journal,* September 1991, 80.

5. Frey and Langseth, *Crying, The Mystery of Tears,* 17.

6. Ronald M. Doctor and Ada P. Kahn, *The Encyclopedia of Phobias, Fears, and Anxieties* (New York: Facts on File, 1989), 120

7. Frey and Langseth, *Crying, The Mystery of Tears,* 71.

8. Gini Kopechy, "Have a Good Cry," *Redbook,* May 1992, 106.

9. Frey and Langseth, *Crying, The Mystery of Tears,* 108.

10. Kopechy, "Have a Good Cry," *Redbook.*

11. Ibid.

12. Frederick S. Perls, M.D., Ralph F. Hefferline and Paul Goodman, *Gestalt Therapy: Excitement and Growth in the Human Personality* (New York: Bantam Books, 1951), 141.

13. Paul Le Tan, *Encyclopedia of 7,700 Illustrations* (Rockville, Md.: Assurance Publishers, Ministers' Research Service, 1984), 1431.

14. *Doland's Illustrated Medical Dictionary* (Philadelphia, Pa.: W. B. Saunders Company: Harcourt Brace Jovanovich, Inc., 1994), 874.

15. "Current Medical Diagnosis and Treatment," *Lange Medical Books* (Stamford, Conn.: Appleton & Lange Publishers, 1992), 129.

16. Ibid.

17. Frey and Langseth, *Crying, The Mystery of Tears,* 108.

18. Ibid.

19. Editors of Prevention Magazine, *Prevention's New Encyclopedia of Common Diseases* (Emmaus, Pa.: Rodale Press, 1984), 916.

20. Frey and Langseth, *Crying, The Mystery of Tears,* 108.

21. Thomas Fuller, *Good Thoughts in Bad Times and Other Papers* (Boston, Mass.: Ticknor and Fields, 1863), 336.

Chapter Six
Something to Cry About

1. David Foster of Associated Press, 15 November 1993.
2. J. H. Jowett, *The Passion for Souls* (New York: Fleming H. Revell Company, 1905), 35.
3. Minnie Lindsay Carpenter, *William Booth: The Founder of The Salvation Army* (London: Wyvern Books, The Epworth Press, 1944).

Chapter Seven
Weeping Through the Word

1. Frank S. Mead, *12,000 Religious Quotations* (Baker Book House, 1989), 34.
2. George Gilfillan, *The Bards of the Bible* (New York: D. Appleton & Co., 1851), 219-220.
3. Poem by Benjamin Beddome.
4. James Strong, *Strong's Exhaustive Concordance of the Bible* (Nashville, Tenn.: Thomas Nelson Publishers, 1984), s.v. "klaio."
5. John P. Gulliver, "Serious Meditations Upon the Four Last Things of Hell and the Estate of Those that Perish," *The Complete Works of John Bunyan: D.D., LL.D* (Brantford, Ontario: Bradley, Garretson & Co., 1881), 994-995.
6. Poem by Benjamin Beddome.

Chapter Eight
Travailing Tears

1. The letter was written by five teenage girls who had given their lives to Christ at the crusade and who themselves are involved in the new church.
2. E. Denny, "To Calvary," *Redemption Hymnal* (Sussex, England: The Joint Redemption Hymnal Committee, Kingsway Publications LTD, 1951), 179.
3. Sharon Begley, "One Pill Makes You Larger, One Pill Makes You Small," *Newsweek,* 7 February 1994, 40.
4. J. H. Jowett, *The Passion for Souls* (New York: Fleming H. Revell Company, 1905), 34.
5. Leonard Ravenhill, *Why Revival Tarries* (Minneapolis, Minn.: Bethany Fellowship, 1959), 132.
6. Ibid., 134.
7. Charles G. Finney, *Lectures on Revivals of Religion* (Oberlin, Ohio: E. J. Goodrich, 1868), 15.
8 Ibid.

9. W. E. Vine, *An Expository Dictionary of New Testament Words* (Fleming H. Revell Company), 151.

10. John E. Smith, ed., *Jonathan Edwards' Works,* vol. 4 (New Haven, Conn.: Yale University Press, 1957), 94.

11. J. William Jones, *Christ in the Camp, or Religion in Lee's Army* (Richmond. Va.: B. F. Johnson & Company, 1887), 202-203.

12. Ravenhill, *Why Revival Tarries,* 137.

Chapter Ten
Tears of Repentance

1. Richard Foster, *Prayer* (San Francisco, Calif.: Harper & Row, 1992), 41.

2. Henry Scougal, *The Life of God in the Soul of Man* (Harrisonburg, Va.: Sprinkle Publications, 1986). 129.

3. Ibid.

4. Jonathan Edwards, *The Life of David Brainerd* (New York: American Tract Society, c. 1833), 154.

5. Edna Dean Proctor and A. Moore, *Life Thoughts, Gathered from the Extemporaneous Discourses of Henry Ward Beecher* (n.p., 1858), 25.

Chapter Eleven
Tears in a Bottle

1. "The Biblical Treasury of Expositions and Illustrations," *London Sunday School Union,* vol. 5 (London: William Rider and Sons Printers, n.d.), 180-181.

2. Maggie Ross, *The Fountain and the Furnace, The Ways of Tears and Fire* (New York: Mahwah Paulist Press, 1987), 159.

3. Joseph Parker, *The Peoples' Bible Discourses Upon Holy Scripture* (London and New York: Funk & Wagnalls, n.d.), 112.

4. Ibid.

5. DeWitt Talmage, quoted by R. M. Offord, ed., "Life's Golden Lamp," *New York Observer,* 1888.

6. Edward Irving, quoted by Elon Foster, *6000 Sermon Illustrations;* previously published as *New Cyclopedia of Prose Illustrations* (Grand Rapids, Mich.: Baker Book House, 1952), 617.

7. Hugh Cleveland, *Bottle Pricing Guide* (Paducah, Ky.: Collector Books; a Division of Schroeder Publishing Company, Inc., 1980), 4.

8. Ibid.

9. W. Robertson Nicoll, ed., "The Psalms by Reverend Alexander MacLaren," *The Expositor's Bible,* vol. 3 (Chicago, Ill.: W. P. Blessing Co., n.d.), 149.

10. John Howie, *The Scots Worthies: Their Lives and Testimonies* (London, Glasgow and Edinburgh: Blackie and Son, 1879), 580-582.

11. C. H. Spurgeon, *The Treasury of David,* vol. 3, 44.

12. Fred W. Krummacher, *The Suffering Saviour or Meditations on the Last Days of Christ,* trans. Samuel Jackson (Boston, Mass.: Gould and Lincoln Publishers, 1859), 193.

Chapter Twelve
Weeping in the Fields

1. Bonar, *Memoirs and Remains.*

2. *The Biblical Treasury: An Illustrative Companion to the Bible,* vol. 5 (London: Sunday School Union, William Rider & Sons), 247.

3. W. M. Thompson, *The Land and the Book* (n.p., n.d.), 21.

4. Helen Spurrell, *A Translation of the Old Testament Scriptures* (London: James Nisbet & Company), 546.

5. George Horne, "A Commentary on the Psalms," quoted in Spurgeon, *Treasury of David,* 22.

6. Philip Doddridge, *Rise and Progress of Religion in the Soul* (New York: American Tract Society, 1840), 206.

7. George Gallup, Jr. and Jim Castelli, *The People's Religion; American Faith in the Nineties* (New York: Macmillan Publishing Company, 1989), 14.

8. Ibid.

9. J. H. Jowett, *Thirsting for the Springs* (New York: George H. Doran Company, n.d.), 165.

10. Dr. Ian R. K. Paisley, *The "Fifty-Nine" Revival* (Belfast, N. Ireland: Martyrs Memorial Free Presbyterian Church, 1959), 185.

11. John Gillies, *Historical Collections of Accounts of Revival* (Edinbugh: Banner of Truth Trust; first published in 1754 by John Gillies and later reprinted in 1845 by Horatius Bonar), 144.

12. Ian Macpherson, *The Burden of the Lord* (Nashville, Tenn.: Abingdon Press, 1955), 12.

13. Joseph Belcher, *George Whitefield, A Biography* (New York: The American Tract Society, 1857), 482-483.

14. Watchman Nee, *The Normal Christian Life* (Wheaton, Ill.: Tyndale House Publishers, 1983).

15. Jonathan Edwards, abridged by John Wesley, *The Work of the Holy Spirit in the Human Heart* (New York: Carlton and Phillips, 1853), 176-177.

16. Bonar, *Memoirs and Remains.*

17. Helen C. Knight, comp., *Lady Huntington and Her Friends* (New York: American Tract Society, 1853), 7.